CW01082122

Writers of Wales

Editors
MEIC STEPHENS   R. BRINLEY JONES

R. Brinley Jones

WILLIAM
SALESBURY

University of Wales Press

Cardiff 1994

I

William Salesbury, second son of Annes and Ffwg
Salesbury – a variant of the form 'Salisbury' – was
born sometime before 1520 in the parish of Llansannan in Denbighshire. His father was of a cadet
branch of the Salisburys of Llewenni, a family of
yeoman stock of English provenance. As a result of
hard work and diplomatic marriages, the Salisburys
had reached positions of influence by the sixteenth
century: in an age of pedigree-consciousness they
were even found noble lineage descending from a
Duke of Bavaria! Ffwg Salesbury died in 1520 and
William's elder brother died twenty years later; by
then, William had moved to Plas Isa, Llanrwst, and
settled there. It was a place described by the poet
Gruffudd Hiraethog as *fair Llanrwst*; Sir John Wynn,
lawyer, scholar, patron, Renaissance gentleman,
recorded how Llanrwst had seen rebellion and how
the market-place had become overgrown and the
churchyard frequented by deer.

In Wales, the century preceding William Salesbury's
birth had certainly known much of the devastation –
and of the economic and social consequences – of
rebellion, in the wake of Owain Glyndŵr's call to *free
the Welsh people from the slavery of their English enemies.*
Wales had also suffered from plague, from loss of life
in the Hundred Years War and the Wars of the
Roses, from disastrous harvests, from lawlessness
and disorder and from a breakdown of administration. The haven of religious houses had been dis-
rupted and this contributed to a decline in the

patronage of culture – of literature in particular. By the end of the fifteenth century, however, there were signs of change: the economy – based on peasant farming, on cloth, leather, dairy produce, woodlands, fisheries, brewing, milling, sheep-rearing and horse-breeding – was improving. Towns were showing signs of greater prosperity and there was less disorder.

But Wales lacked the outward symbols of nationhood; it had no capital city, no royal court. With Glyndŵr's passing had disappeared, for the time being, the notion of creating a Welsh university. Communication within Wales was not good; the country, on the whole, consisted of isolated pastoral communities and small towns. (The gentry had been extending their estates and were to add still further to them when the monasteries were dissolved.) But when Henry Tudor landed near Milford Haven in 1485 and led a march through Wales to defeat Richard III at Bosworth, there were new hopes among the Welsh. Within half a century the Acts of Union formalized the relationship between Wales and the Crown and allowed the Welsh gentry to increase their prosperity. The classical Renaissance, the Protestant Reformation and the Union, between them, were to alter the subsequent history of Wales. It was Salesbury's good fortune to be born into this period of change: it was the great fortune of Wales that he – among others – was there to accept and answer the challenge . . . and to do so with sensitivity and an awareness of the past, grafting the new on to the old. The doyen of Welsh historians, Professor Glanmor Williams, has labelled the period 1415–1536 as 'Rebellion and Recovery: the Twilight of Medieval Wales'. Salesbury was to see the dawn of a new age.

Of Salesbury's boyhood we know little except that, on his own evidence, he was at one time in Lancashire. Did he attend school there, or did he go to a parish, town or private venture school nearer home? Was it his school experience that he called upon when he wrote, in 1550, *Nowe I truste that the dullest wytted chyld that neuer reade but two lynes, perceaueth so familiar a rudimente?* Sir John Wynn, born in 1553, relates how his great grandfather had been to school at Caernarfon *where he learnt the English tongue, to read, to write, to understand Latin, a matter of great moment in those days.* Were the family connections good enough or the boy William Salesbury promising enough to have placed him in the charge of an educated clergyman – not that there were very many of them? Though the Abbey of Aberconwy at Maenan, a short distance away from Salesbury's home, was by now in a state of serious decline, was there someone left capable of giving him instruction? After all, Hugh Price (who died in 1528), who had become abbot when still a minor and had been educated at Cambridge, was brother to Catrin Llwyd, later to become Salesbury's wife. We do not know, but one thing is certain: whatever kind of formal education he received, the inspiration he gained from the literary associations of his locality were great and lasting. Llansannan had been the birth-place of Tudur Aled (*c.* 1465–*c.* 1525) in whose work the bardic tradition reached its apogee and who had composed an elegy in honour of Salesbury's great grandfather and an eulogy of his grandfather. The Vale of Clwyd had a tradition of literary activity unsurpassed in the whole of Wales; it was a region that had nurtured and conserved a host of literary talents. Indeed it became a veritable archive of Welsh literary treasure. It had been the home of the *penceirddiaid Cymraeg*, the Welsh 'chiefs of song', at the end of the Middle Ages and it became the centre of Welsh Renaissance activity. The old and the new met there. Gruffudd Hiraethog, born towards the close of the fifteenth century, a pupil of Tudur Aled and one of the major poets of his time, inherited the craft of the bardic schools; he was to be the link between that bardic learning and the new writing of the Renaissance found in William Salesbury's work. Little wonder that Salesbury was to refer to the poets as *penseiri yr iaith*, 'architects of the language'. He was much obligated to his friend Gruffudd Hiraethog for communicating to him the secrets of bardic craft and the vocabulary of earlier Welsh writing. Formal schooling apart, William Salesbury was superbly placed to be aware of the wealth of the Welsh literary heritage; it was a wealth that he was to build upon vigorously.

Like so many of his contemporaries anxious to further their studies, Salesbury proceeded to Oxford. Several of his fellow countrymen were to distinguish themselves in their various fields: William Thomas (hanged in 1554 for conspiring to assassinate Queen Mary), clerk of the Privy Council, author of the first book (1550) in English to treat of the grammar of the Italian language and of the first Italian-English dictionary, and also of a HISTORIE OF ITALY (1549); Robert Recorde (d. 1558), mathematician and physician; Sir Edward Carne (*c.* 1500–1561), lawyer and diplomat; Richard Davies (*c.* 1501–1581), bishop and biblical translator, who translated, for example, the Epistles of 1 Timothy, Hebrews, James and 1 and 2 Peter in the 1567 Welsh edition of the New Testament but also the books between Joshua and 2 Samuel into English for the 'Bishop's Bible' of 1568;

Sir John Price (*c*. 1502–1555), notary public and scholar, who was responsible for the first printed and published book in Welsh, YN Y LHYVYR HWNN, of 1546; Gruffydd Robert (pre-1532–post-1598), Roman Catholic priest and author of the first grammar of the Welsh language to be written in Welsh; Morys Clynnog (*c*. 1525–1581), Roman Catholic theologian; Humphrey Lhuyd (1527–1568), antiquary, author, map-maker, member of Parliament; Siôn Dafydd Rhys (1534–*c*. 1619), physician and grammarian of Welsh published in Latin, of Latin published in Italian and author of a short work in Latin on the pronunciation and orthography of Italian; Sir Thomas Wiliems (*c*. 1545–*c*. 1622), priest, manuscript copyist and collector, lexicographer and physician. There were others too, of course, true products of the breadth of Renaissance curiosity and scholarship.

According to Anthony Wood, the Oxford chronicler, Salesbury probably resided in Broadgates Hall; as a student he would have followed a curriculum largely unchanged over the years, based on the Trivium and Quadrivium, which is described in detail by the Cardiganshire gentleman poet Ieuan ap Rhydderch (fl. 1430–1470) in 'Y Fost', 'The Boast'. In his DICTION-ARY of 1547 Salesbury lists *arithmetik astronomi music* among the *seven arts* and in 1550 he refers to *the preceptes of Grāmer*; Gruffudd Hiraethog comments on Salesbury's mastery of the arts. The University was slow to shed old traditions and although Scholasticism was in decline, it was still the backbone of academic discipline and methodology. Salesbury's use of the word *Dilechtid* (deriving from *Dialectica*) to express 'guile' and 'craftiness' in 1567 may well indicate that the divisions of medieval instruction were disintegrating.

5

There were new ideas and methods on the way. Already by the middle of the fifteenth century there was a new library developing above the Divinity School at Oxford; it consisted of a collection of books presented by Humphrey, duke of Gloucester, youngest son of Henry IV. The duke had enjoyed close contact with many Italian humanists and between 1435 and 1444 he had presented some 280 manuscripts to the library, many of them classical and humanist texts. In 1431 Duke Humphrey had commented on the curriculum, suggesting *a new emphasis (be) given to the study of rhetoric and classical literature.* There was by the middle of the century a nucleus of classical texts in the library, and with the advent of printing and a growing interest in the business of authorship the collection grew and grew. The printing press had come to Oxford before the end of the fifteenth century; in 1478 a commentary on the *Credo* was printed there – though London was the centre of printing. By the time Salesbury was a student there was no shortage of material and no lack of desire to study it. Scholars had been caught up in the renaissance of learning which was burgeoning in Europe and a whole group of them came or returned to Oxford fired with excitement over texts and exegesis, men like Grocyn, Linacre, Colet, More, Vives and above all Erasmus, *the head learned man of all our tyme,* as Salesbury described him in 1550. Their teaching was to inspire generation after generation. When Corpus Christi College was founded in 1517 it had been Richard Fox's aim that it would cater for the new studies: the Foundation Statutes had spoken of *a beehive . . . whose scholars like clever bees will day and night make wax to the honour of God and sweet honey for their own profit and that of all Christians.* This kind of busyness, usefulness, taste, was to inspire Salesbury: Oxford gave him a grounding in the traditional learning of the University, but he felt the winds of change sweeping across Europe and recognized the immense potential of the printing press. He was to employ the press to a greater extent than any of his contemporaries in Wales.

In addition Oxford challenged the religious observance of his youth and planted the seeds of Protestantism in his heart and mind. In this challenge he was the inheritor of the tradition of Christian humanism exemplified in the works and teaching of Erasmus and Colet who examined the Scriptures with the care and precision they and their humanist forebears had exercised in respect of classical texts. There was a determination to return *ad fontes*. The medieval Church, Pope-dominated, Latin in language, sacramental in worship, clerical and hierarchical, was being subjected to scrutiny. William Salesbury had been, in his own words, *tangeled, and abhominablye deceyved, and trayned, and brought vp in tender age, in the Popes holilyke Religion before Christes seconde byrthe here in Englande*. It was probably *here in Englande* at Oxford that he first felt the pangs and thrills of that *seconde byrthe*. Language study was providing more than textual criticism; it was penetrating the very essence of dogma.

Had Oxford also given him a taste for other languages? In 1574 Sir Thomas Wiliems said of him, *W.S. . . . is the most learned Briton not only in British, but also in Hebrew, Greek, Latin, English, French, German, and other languages* (tr.). And although in his 'letter' to John Edwardes of Chirk in 1550, Salesbury declared *where as Englysshe to me of late yeares was wholy to lerne, the Latyn not tasted of, the Greke not once*

7

harde of and he did not *professe the perfect phrase of any of theym*, evidence in his work suggests a considerable interest in and knowledge of languages. In 1547, in describing the characteristics of the consonants *m* and *n* in English, he says they are identical with the sounds in Welsh, *yes and in every language of which I have knowledge* (tr.): he refers to Latin, Greek, Hebrew and even recalls an Anglo-Saxon usage – the runic letter 'thorn', which he had heard from *hen ddarlleydd o sais* ('an aged English reader'). He refers to the 'thorn' again in 1550 in A BRIEFE AND A PLAYNE INTRODUCTION, TEACHYNG HOW TO PRONOUNCE THE LETTERS IN THE BRITISH TONG, and displays acquaintance with Hebrew, Greek, Latin, French, German, Spanish and 'Scottish'. He comments: *For in readynge Englyshe or Frenche, ye do not reade some wordes all so fully as they be wrotē.* Even in Y LLYSIEULYFR, the herbal on which he worked between 1568 and 1574, he lists equivalent forms in other languages, such as *Succisa in Latin, Divels bytte in English, caswenwyn in Welsh . . . teuffels abbiffy the people of Germany . . . Mord de Diable, the French* (tr.). (Doubtless the incorrect German and French forms are attributable to a later copyist.)

Might it have been at Oxford, too, that he witnessed what the devotees of the other vernaculars were doing for their own, and that, there, he gained a new vision and a new conviction concerning his own obligation to Wales and Welsh? The *questione della lingua* had been a debate in Italy, France and England. With the new desire to make Scripture and 'learning' accessible to the people, knowledge of the vernaculars – including Welsh for the Welsh – assumed a new significance. Scholarship and printing were at hand to make such accessibility a reality. In the Middle Ages, Wales had been part of the *Respublica Christiana*; the changes, imminent by Salesbury's time, were to cause some separation. But Oxford may well have taught him of the *Respublica Litterarum* of which Wales must be part. And was it at Oxford, too, that he realized that since *sola Scriptura* was the refrain of Protestantism, it was urgently necessary to give vernaculars the respect and cultivation that they needed in order to advance the cause of Protestantism?

No record exists of his having taken a degree at Oxford, but there was nothing particularly unusual about that. Many young men entered the university without thought of taking a degree, merely to enjoy the benefit of a year or two of advanced education, or to follow a fashion, as in the case of Sir Roger Williams (*c.* 1540–1595) of Penrhos, Monmouth, who sought and found fame and fortune in the European wars, and who was *from his childhood more given to military than scholastical matters, yet for form's sake he was sent to the university* (as Anthony Wood said of him). Others proceeded to other professions or to the Inns of Court.

There is no reference to Salesbury's having been a member of one of the Inns though we know he was at Thavies Inn in London in 1550; Thavies was one of the Inns of Chancery founded by a Welshman, John Davy, in the fourteenth century. There are, however, clear indications in his work that he was conversant with legal matters and we know that he was serving Sir Richard Rich, the Lord Chancellor, in 1550. There is reference to his having been involved in lawsuits, one a family dispute, one of assault in which the notorious Dr Elis Prys, 'the red doctor', Salesbury's

brother-in-law, was implicated. In 1550 in A BRIEFE
AND A PLAYNE INTRODUCTION . . . he says, *For I do
remembre that once a clarke (being but a yonge begynner)
at an assise in oure countrye, redde a mans name beinge
(shorte written) Eden ap Iorum wher he should haue read
it Edenyuet ap Yorwerth.* (In the 1567 edition of the
book, Denbigh is named as the place where this
occurred.)

There is no reference, either, to Salesbury's having
travelled abroad as so many of his contemporaries
were to do. He spent some considerable time in
London supervising the printing of his works
as when he was *soiourning at your house in Paules
Churchyarde*, as he says, referring to the house of
Humphrey Toy, the bookseller. In 1550 he remarks
*And I myselfe haue hearde Englyshmen in some contryes
of Englaude sounde f. euen as we sounde it in Walshe*
. . . During the reign of Catholic Mary, when his
caution and family connections probably afforded
him protection, he was most likely back in Llanrwst
reading and preparing himself for his life's work. His
comment in 1547 that there was *hardly a parish in
Wales without English people in it* (tr.) and his knowledge of dialect forms might suggest that he was
already acquainted with various regions of his native
country, unless it was that he acquired such information from others whom he met. We know that he
enjoyed the hospitality of Bishop Richard Davies at
Abergwili between 1564 and 1566 while they were
collaborating on the translation of the Prayer Book
and New Testament which appeared in 1567. Davies
will have told him of the years of his exile, 1555 to
1558, at Frankfurt am Main, that centre of Protestant
activity and of lively interest in learning and the
power of the printing press. But somewhere, earlier,

he had acquired first-hand information about German: in 1550 he says, *For althoughe the Germaynes vse a w, yet in some wordes sound they it (to my hearing) as the forther u, were a vowell, and the latter a consonant.*

William Salesbury married Catrin Llwyd, sister to Elis Prys, and although there is reference to their having separated at one stage, the poet Wiliam Cynwal, in an elegy composed on Catrin in about 1572, refers to the sore loss to her husband *Y braw tost i briod hon.* They had three children. We do not know the date of Salesbury's death though it is now assumed that he may well have died in about 1580. (There is a reference in THE HISTORY OF THE GWYDIR FAMILY by Sir John Wynn that he lived until 1599.) It seems that his passing was unsung by the poets: at least, no record survives. His memorial is his extraordinary service to Welsh letters.

Such service was rendered possible by Salesbury's early realization that the resources of the Welsh language needed to be marshalled and used to their maximum. He dedicated his life to rendering the Renaissance and Reformation intelligible to his fellow countrymen. He collected proverbs and prepared a dictionary: he looked critically at the language, he collected and coined terms of Rhetoric. But his horizons were those of the new men of the Renaissance: he translated a scientific work into English and a medicinal herbal into Welsh. Above all, however, he was a Protestant and a Welsh one at that: the LESSONS AND ARTICLES OF HOLY SCRIPTURE of 1551, the PRAYER BOOK and NEW TESTAMENT of 1567 are essentially his. For almost thirty years he was to be the ear and mouthpiece of the Renaissance and Reformation in Wales.

II

The mechanical device of printing was the major instrument in revolutionizing man's vision of God and of his fellow human beings in the sixteenth century. It was to open the doors of literature and thought, it was to make the Scriptures available and ultimately accessible. There was, as has been stated, a return to fundamentals, and a scrutiny of texts – pagan and Christian – was to occupy the minds of thinking men. Curiosity and respect for the 'word' in exact translation of classical texts and Scripture were hallmarks of the time. The first book to be printed in these islands appeared in 1477 and emanated from William Caxton's press which had been set up in the precincts of Westminster Abbey: a year later Theodoric Rood from Cologne printed at Oxford the Commentary on the Apostles' Creed attributed to St Jerome. It was almost seventy years later that the first printed book appeared in Welsh – YN Y LHYVYR HWNN, a collection of devotional material by Sir John Price of Brecon; it appeared in 1546, printed in London by Edward Whitchurch. But soon to follow were books by William Salesbury and others in Welsh and English, reflecting the avid interest of the times in *litterae sacrae* and *litterae humaniores*. No one more than Salesbury exploited the potential of the press for the service of the Welsh people in the sixteenth century. This exploitation was to change the mind and the soul of Wales.

It is not surprising that among his first printed books should be a dictionary: such a publication could open the door to knowledge over a wide variety of areas. Salesbury's work, A DICTIONARY IN ENGLYSHE AND WELSHE, appeared in 1547, printed by John Waley *at London in Foster Lane*. It ends with a greeting from the printer:

Behold kind Welshmen I have come and printed a small number of these books at the behest of a gentleman of your country who testified that I would find you such ready bargainers such agreeable companions and so courteous in fellowship, that I would not regret taking such pain and travail and cost on your behalf. (tr.)

The title-page states that the book is issued by the authority of the king: prefixed to the dictionary is *a litle treatyse of the englyshe pronunciacion of the letters*. There is a dedicatory letter to Henry VIII, *your excellent wysdome . . . hath causede to be enactede . . . that there shal herafter be no difference in lawes and language bytwyxte youre subiectes of youre principalytye of Wales and your other subiectes*. The author continues, *. . . what a bonde and knotte of loue and frendshyppe the communion of one tonge is*.

The art of printing exposed the 'word', gave it sanction and definition *pro tempore*; it was the work of the dictionary to give it an imprimatur. The first recorded example of the word 'dictionary' in English appears in 1526 and the first time it was used in a title of a book was in the Latin–English publication of 1538, THE DICTIONARY OF SYR THOMAS ELIOT KNYGHT, the chief source of which had been the Latin DICTIONARIUM of Ambrosius Calepinus of Bergamo. It took Eliot two years to prepare and by the year of his death three editions had appeared. The first Latin–English dictionary to be published was [H]ORT-US VOCABULORUM, printed by Wynkyn de Worde in

1500 (and this went into many editions – maybe as many as twelve – by 1533). In 1499 there had appeared a Breton–French–Latin dictionary by Jehan Lagadeuc which he had completed in 1464. There was a passion for words which continued throughout the period of the Renaissance: discovery of past literature, translating Scripture, expression of new ideas all called for new symbols and it was imperative that, in an age which not only extended the boundaries of knowledge but which desired accessibility to it, there should be an explanation of the meaning of words. Salesbury shared this passion and this desire to open the minds and the hearts of his fellow countrymen. Andrew Borde in his Fyrst Boke of the Introduction of Knowledge, published in about 1547, included a specimen of Gypsy language, and *The Second chapter treateth of the naturall dysposicion of Walshmen and of the countre of Wales techi'g an Englyshe man to speake some walshe.* It is suggested that Borde may have been, for a time, in London in 1547 – the year of Salesbury's Dictionary – overseeing the publication of his books. Borde's Astronamye *I dyd wrett and make . . . in iiii dayes, and wretten with one old pen with out mendyng.* There was an urgency about publication.

William Salesbury may well have been acquainted with these works: certainly he shared the urgency and perhaps rushed into print, sometimes *with out mendyng*, or to use a phrase from his dictionary, *ar vrys* 'in haste'. His dictionary has many gaps – some of them inexplicable in that, for example, *ymyrus* is followed by a blank but is translated as 'busy' in the introductory treatise. In the preliminaries is found *tentes, pepyll*, but not in the dictionary. And there are words which appear in his letter to 'the Welsh reader' which prefaced OLL SYNNWYR PEN KEMBERO YGYD, published also in 1547, which find no place in the dictionary. The gaps almost look ready for additions in a way that manuscript lists had afforded: the DICTIONARY has something of the nature of a work-book, devised in the first place for his own use: that might explain why the order of words is Welsh–English though the title-page suggests otherwise. Maybe the permanence of the printed word had hardly been realized: the introductory treatise on learning to read English has a quality of first draft about it – *But pardon the length of this exposition: I shall sooner be brief for those letters that remain* (tr.). Salesbury was certainly acquainted with the Welsh manuscript vocabularies and utilized them for his own purpose – just as the first English–Latin dictionary, the PROMPTORIUM PARVULORUM, the first printed edition of which appeared in 1499, was indebted to the many English–Latin and Latin–English word-lists in manuscript in the fourteenth and fifteenth centuries.

Clearly the purpose of Salesbury's DICTIONARY was to acquaint those whose first language was Welsh with English equivalents for Welsh words; English was *a language, today, adorned with all manner of learning* (tr.). The apparent contradiction of his desire on the one hand for his fellow countrymen to learn English and, on the other, his devotion to Welsh and his conviction of the importance of providing Scripture and secular literature in Welsh, has presented scholars with something of a dilemma. The explanation may well be that Salesbury, Tudor Welshman as he was, saw the urgency of his fellow countrymen's plight: English had already achieved success in facing the demands of the new 'culture'. Salesbury

15

was young when he prepared his dictionary: as soon as he perceived how Welsh could meet the demands of that 'culture', he devoted his talent and his energy to writing in Welsh.

The DICTIONARY includes words which, by Salesbury's time, were archaic; it includes a cross-section of current vocabulary, dialect forms, English borrowings and words he noted from the bardic vocabularies which were part of the apparatus of the professional poets. The DICTIONARY mirrors something of the times: among many, many, others there are words for white barley, rye, oat and brown bread, home-made cloth, Irish rug, trout, bullock, palmistry, physiognomy, counterfeit hair, glover, white lime, minstrel, righteousness, Paris candle, carpet, beggar, venison, claret, cobbler, copper, lawyer, lantern, Latinist, dyer, forgiveness, Mars, strawberries, parchment, doublet, martyr, chivalry, money, blackberry, Homer, frying-pan, sermon, robbery, satin of Bruges, satin of Cyprus, spectacles, tennis, rape, witchcraft, butter, divorce, historiographer. The occasional departure from a short definition affords a sly humour, as when he treats *wynwyn* 'an onion', and adds, in Welsh, *a herb which women put to their eyes to produce weeping when their husbands die.*

By the end of the sixteenth century, after Salesbury's work and that of many of the other biblical translators, humanist writers and scholars had done, the language had been stretched even further: such contortions and exposure called for a major dictionary with a new imprimatur. It appeared in the form of a Welsh–Latin and Latin–Welsh dictionary (the latter a shortened version of a work by Thomas Wiliems, Trefriw, itself based on the DICTIONARIUM

LINGUAE LATINAE ET ANGLICANAE by Thomas Thomas, first printer to the University of Cambridge), by Dr John Davies, rector of Mallwyd; it was published in 1632, the crown of humanist scholarship in Wales. But Salesbury was the pioneer of the printed lexicon. Wales had to wait until 1688 for its next Welsh–English dictionary (Y GYMRAEG YN EI DISGLEIR-DEB by Thomas Jones). Defective and incomplete though Salesbury's DICTIONARY is, it remains a monument to his research instinct, his taste for words, his concern for literacy and ultimately his endeavour to offer a key to the understanding of Scripture.

III

The period 1547 to 1552 was intensely active for Salesbury. Here is a list of the publications of those years:

1547 A DICTIONARY IN ENGLYSHE AND WELSHE
1547 OLL SYNNWYR PEN KEMBERO YGYD
1550 A BRIEFE AND A PLAYNE INTRODUCTION, TEACH-
YNG HOW TO PRONOUNCE THE LETTERS IN THE
BRITISH TONG . . .
1550 THE DESCRIPCION OF THE SPHERE OR FRAME OF
THE WORLDE
1550 BAN WEDY I DYNNY AIR YNGAIR ALLAN O HEN
GYFREITH HOWEL DDA
1550 THE BATERIE OF THE POPES BOTEREULX
1551 KYNNIVER LLITH A BAN
(1552: in manuscript, 'Llyfr Rhetoreg').

As the list shows, within the same year as the DIC-
TIONARY appeared Salesbury was responsible for the publication of OLL SYNNWYR PEN KEMBERO YGYD, 'The Summa of a Welshman's Wisdom' (tr.). It was printed *at London in saynt Iohns strete by Nycholas Hyll* and was a collection of some nine hundred and thirty proverbs which Salesbury claimed he had taken *by stealth* from a manuscript copy in the hand of Gruffudd Hiraethog. Proverbs were much in vogue both here and in other parts of Europe. Thomas Eliot in the Preface to his DICTIONARY had stated: *Nor I haue omitted prouerbes, whiche I thought necessarie to be had in remembraunce.* They were from the ADAGIA and APOPHTHEGMATA of Erasmus. The letter to the Welsh reader introducing OLL SYNNWYR PEN is Salesbury's; it has been described by Saunders

Lewis as the manifesto of the Renaissance of learning and of Welsh Protestant humanism and in it Salesbury refers to Erasmus, John Heywood and Polydore Vergil and their compilations of proverbs.

James Howell, the writer born in 1593 in Abernant, Carmarthenshire, author of the LEXICON TETRA-GLOTTON (1659–1660), an English–French–Italian–Spanish dictionary, describes proverbs as possessing *shortness, sense and salt*. In Salesbury's letter he refers to them as being *short, sensible, counselling sayings* (tr.). They record the wisdom of the ages: *What are proverbs but some sparks of the immeasureable wisdom of God?*(tr.), is how he puts it. Certainly there was a long tradition of proverb-collecting in Welsh, as Salesbury reminds us. The oldest collection is to be found in the Black Book of Chirk, a manuscript dating from the middle of the thirteenth century which also includes the oldest Welsh text of the Laws of Hywel Dda. There are collections, too, in the White Book of Rhydderch (that invaluable collection of Welsh medieval prose including the Mabinogion, other romances and religious writing) dating from the middle of the fourteenth century, and the Red Book of Hergest, a remarkable miscellany of Welsh writing, dating from the end of the fourteenth century. There is no doubt that Gruffudd Hiraethog had based his collection on material he had found in earlier manuscripts, and Salesbury acknowledges Gruffudd's service to the language in making such a compilation and in other ways, and invites his fellow countrymen to sustain him in his efforts.

Why did Salesbury think it necessary to publish such a collection? There were several reasons: the fashion of the times, the fact that they represented the *sapientia* (*eneit yr iaith*, 'the soul of the language') so much respected in the Renaissance mind, and that they provided the vocabulary ingredients necessary for other works. *Are not proverbs the same support to the language as bones are to the body? Do not proverbs supply the same beauty to language, as stars to the firmament?* (tr.), is how he measures their value. It is Salesbury's contention that *I myself and a thousand Welshmen will find instruction, benefit and consolation* (tr.) from reading them.

But there is a wider *cri de coeur* in the letter. He begs those who possess manuscripts of all kinds to make them available: they will be invaluable resources of vocabulary for the great tasks ahead. If such were made known to scholars it would be *easier for a learned Welshman, having been away from his country, and having lost command of his language, to translate from another language into ours* (tr.). And above all, the vocabulary of such works of the past would serve well in the work of Scripture translation. *Because, since you hide the old books in your language, and particularly those of Holy Scripture, there is no Welshman alive, however learned he be, who can treat properly the Holy Scripture in Welsh* (tr.). The language, he says, needs cultivation: the everyday vocabulary of *buying, selling, eating and drinking* is inadequate and will need *more words, more phrases* (tr.) to meet the new demands. *If there is no learning, knowledge, wisdom, godliness in a language, it is hardly better than the chatter of wild birds* (tr.). Wisdom apart, there is the pressing need of saving the souls of his fellow countrymen; he implores Welshmen: *Demand the Holy Scripture in your language, as it was with your blessed forebears, the Old British* (tr.). The Welsh have been deprived of some of their former glory and are *aliens* in their own land. Then he addresses the dilemma precisely. *Make pilgrimage, barefoot, to the King's majesty and his Council to solicit to have leave for the Holy Scripture in your language, for the sake of those of you who are neither able nor likely to learn English* (tr.). By hook or by crook, Salesbury was determined to carry Wales into the new age, and to do so with urgency.

The contents of OLL SYNNWYR PEN were reprinted with corrections and additions, together with other material including the 'Triads of the Island of Britain', in 1567. Only one copy of that edition exists and that is imperfect. The title was probably CRYNODAB OR DIAREBION SATHREDIG: TRIOEDD YNYS PRYDAIN A THALM OR PHILOSOPHI NEVR HEN ATHRONDDYSG CAMBERAIG ('A summary of the common proverbs: Triads of the island of Britain and an extract of the philosophy or old wisdom of the Welsh'). A manuscript copy was made from the book in 1577. Salesbury's purpose in this second edition of 1567, amplified and again much indebted to Gruffudd Hiraethog's work, was to publish some of the traditional lore of the Welsh. William Camden, the distinguished antiquary, was to use the section on the triads, as was Humphrey Lhuyd.

In the dedicatory epistle to Richard Langford, Jancyn Gwyn and Humphrey Lhuyd, *good learned men* (tr.), Salesbury begs for further examples of proverbs. These could be inserted in the gaps allowed (a reminder, maybe, of the gaps in the DICTIONARY). Lhuyd might even supply Italian proverbs. Salesbury recalls how he had seen examples in the Red Book of Hergest *which I saw three years ago last Michaelmas in Ludlow with Sir Harry Sidney, Lord President . . . arranged in alphabetical order* (tr.). Some, Salesbury explains, were included in this present work so that younger scholars might recognize *phrases yr jaith*, 'the phrases of the language'. The refrain is in line with Salesbury's thinking – such collections demonstrate the *sapientia* of the past and provide verbal ammunition for the challenges facing the language in the future.

IV

Salesbury's English works belong (second editions apart) to the year 1550: they include a treatise on the pronunciation of Welsh, a translation of a scientific work, a short bilingual pamphlet on the historical justification for priests marrying and a polemical work on the Mass and stone altars in churches. The extent of his original works in English exceeds that of his Welsh writing.

The first of these English works, known subsequently by its short title, A BRIEFE AND A PLAYNE INTRODUC-TION, was *imprinted at London by Roberte Crowley, dwellyng in Elye rentes in Holburne.* (Modern students of the English and Welsh languages of the sixteenth century have found it to be a work of seminal importance.) The full title sets out, very clearly, the scope of the study:

A briefe and a playne introduction, teachyng how to pronounce the letters in the British tong, (now cōmenly called Walsh) wherby an English man shal not only with ease read the said tong rightly: but markyng ye same wel, it shal be a meaue for him with one labour and diligence to attaine to the true and natural pronunciation of other expediente and most excellente languages . . .

It was basically a phonetic guide to Welsh intended for those border Welsh people whose work *for their promotions and lyuynges* and trade put them in contact with *them that can not a worde of Englishe,* for those exiled who had lost their Welsh but who wished to renew their roots, and for those scholars who had an interest in language, the *philoglottous* as Salesbury says.

There is a dedicatory epistle *To hys louynge frende, maister Rychard Colyngborne,* an address to the reader and at the end a second address to *maister Colingborn* in which Salesbury declares the copiousness of the language in terms reminiscent of his contemporaries in Italy, France and England. Indeed, Salesbury was the example *par excellence* of *défense et illustration* in his theory and practice, as du Bellay was, for example, in France and as others of their contemporaries were in their several countries. The following excerpts from the second address show Salesbury, Tudor Welshman, aware of the achievements of English, conscious of the distinction of the past in Wales: they illustrate, at the same time, his command of the English language.

> *I would fayne wyth all industry endeuer my selfe to helpe and further all Walshemen to come to the knoweledge of Englyshe, as a language moste expediente, aud most worthiest to be learned, studied, and enhaũced, . . . euen for the attaynement of knowledge in Gods word, and other liberall sciences whyche thorowe the benifite of the learned men of our dayes be communely hadde and sette forth in the said Englishe tongue.*
>
> *Agayne as for the Walsh tong euen as it is not now to be compared wyth the Englyshe language, so is it not so rude, so grosse, nor so barbarous, as straũgers beynge therein all ignorante and blynd do adiugde it to be: nor yet (to speake indifferentlye wythout all affections) is it not all so copious, so fyne, so pure, nor so fully replenished with eligancie, graces, & eloquence, as they them selues suppose it.*
>
> *Howebeit whan the whole Isle was communelye called Brytayne, the dwellers Brutes or Brytõs, and accordyngelye their language Brytishe, I wyll not refell nor greatelye denye, neyther can I iustelye gaynsaye but theyr tonge than was as copious of*

24

fit wordes, and all maner of propre vocables, and as well adournated wyth worshypfull sciences, and honorable knoweledge, as anye other barbarous tonges were.

. . . what consonant and fine termes, and what sentencious and net adages, whych the olde, sage, & learned fathers haue not only inuented, but also of the Grekes and the Latines moste prosperouslye haue taken, translated, accepted, and vntill thys daye stil retayned: I wyl omit to declare any white of the manifolde retorical phrases, I wyll winke at the tropes, metaphores, & translations, and such maner of speaches whych the Brytyshe tonge hath as commune, yea rather as peculier or sisterlyke wyth the holy language./The Hebrue tōge . . . the unspekeable felicitie, and the wōderous graces of the Brytishe meters . . .

But now after thys, oh, howe it greaueth me to disclose . . . that there remayneth now but walsh pamphlets for the goodly Brytish bokes, sometyme so well furnished wyth all kynde of literature: and so fewe Brytyshe fragmentes of the booke of Christes owne religion . . .

The bulk of the work is a lesson in pronunciation: *to introducte . . . to pronounce the letters Englyshe like;* it has a short comparative study of Welsh sounds with Hebrew and Greek and *A generall rule for the readynge of Walsh.* The treatment is admirably lucid. Here is Salesbury observant, analytical:

The Walsh man or the Hispanyard compose their mouthes muche after one fashion whā they pronoūce their ll, sauynge that the walsheman vttereth it wyth a more thicker and a more mightier spirite.

For althoughe the Germaynes vse a w, yet in some wordes sound they it (to my hearing) as the forther u, were a vowell, and the latter a consonant . . .

He was the first to treat of the Latin element in Welsh and that in his DICTIONARY of 1547: here he elaborated as he did further in the second edition of A BRIEFE AND A PLAYNE INTRODUCTION.

This revised edition appeared in 1567 under the title A PLAYNE AND A FAMILIAR INTRODUCTION; its title page reads:

This Treatise is most requisite for any man, yea though he can indifferently well reade the tongue, who wyl be thorowly acquainted with anie piece of translation, wherein the sayd Salesbury hath dealed.

And so, the 1567 edition had yet another potential audience – the Welsh themselves. In addition, he was now to rejoice that Wales *shoulde participate and enjoy the incomparable treasure of Christes Euangelie. His long desired peticion* had been answered. Little wonder that his energies henceforth should be channelled into works in Welsh. These we shall examine later, after we have considered the other English writings of 1550.

V

Among the most distinguished Renaissance scholars residing in Oxford at the end of the fifteenth century was Thomas Linacre: he had been elected Fellow of All Souls in 1484, was a friend of Colet, Erasmus and More and had tasted at first hand the stirrings of the Italian Renaissance, having visited Florence, Padua and Rome. He was founder of the Royal College of Physicians and was among the first to cultivate Greek letters in England. In 1500 or 1501 he was called to court as tutor to the young Prince Arthur: some two years earlier he had published DE SPHAERA, his Latin translation from the Greek of Diadochus Proclus. It was this translation which was *Englysshed* by William Salesbury under the title THE DESCRIPCION OF THE SPHERE OR FRAME OF THE WORLDE which appeared in 1550.

The dedicatory letter *To his verye louynge Cosen Iohn Edwardes of Chyrcke* states how Edwards had invited Salesbury *to prouyde you of some Boke, treatynge in Englysshe* on the subject. Salesbury had wandered about St Paul's churchyard *from shop to shop, enquyrynge of such a treatyse.* He found no English work but came across the Latin translation of the Greek original by Proclus, *But wolde God that he, whiche translated it into the Laten, had taken so moche paine, as for his countre sake, as to englysshe the same . . .* So Salesbury proceeded *to translate a Scyence unknowen, out of a tonge unknowen, in to a tonge no better knowen unto me.* He would *wrest it rather than truely tourne it, and that for lacke of farther connynge.* Of John Edwards himself, Salesbury acknowledges, *you stamer some*

The Descripcion of the Sphere or Frame of the Worlde (1550) what both in the Laten tonge, and in this science also. With all Edwards's accomplishments, he was *almost ygnoraunte, (for the seldomnes of the science,) in the speculacion of the wonderfull goodly, and deuyne fabricature of the world* . . . The letter was written *At Thauies Inne in Houlborne. Anno domini 1550.*

In addition to the letter, much in the tradition of the Renaissance prefaces, is an address *To the gentyll Reader*, not only an *apologia* of his own inadequacies or knowledge of the science but also a belief in the generosity of experts in the field in contrast with the writers in some other scientific disciplines. It ends:

Yet because I am in a maner thorowlye perswaded, that the doers in this heavenlye Knowledge, wyll rather gently and brotherly correcte a faulte, where a faulte is, than malyciously espye out two for one I wyll be so unshamefastlye bolde, as to sette before theym, this messe of these my unrype, and fyrste Fruytes, trustynge moche more to their gentlynes, than in the worthynes of the preparacions of theyr Banket.

Despite the protestation of constraint of composition (*out of a tonge unknowen, in to a tonge no better knowen unto me*), Salesbury – as can be recognized from his original writing in English – was not without flair. And apart from thinking of the work as a response to John Edwards's request, Salesbury was beginning to exercise his talents for translation. Maybe the original Proclus was at his disposal as well as the Linacre, and his 'wresting' with the English was preparation in technique for his Scriptural translations.

VI

Also published in 1550, printed by Robert Crowley in London was a pamphlet in Welsh and English, BAN WEDY I DYNNY . . . It quotes from *the auncient lawe of Hoel da, than kynge of Wales, by the whych ye maie easely gather that priests at that time had maried wyues, neither was it prohibited or forbidden by the lawe: whyche Lawe was accepted, confirmed, & auctorized by the bishop of Rome* . . . This was now *the Kynges lawe also*: such a law had been passed in November 1548 – *An Acte to take awaye all posityve Lawes against Marriage of Priestes*. It was Salesbury's contribution to the matter and although his name does not appear in the pamphlet, it was, without doubt, his work.

Another work which appeared in the same year, also emanating from the press of Robert Crowley, *dwelling in Elye rentes in Holbourne*, was THE BATERIE OF THE POPES BOTEREULX, COMMONLYE CALLED THE HIGH ALTARE. It was dedicated to *hys singuler good Lord, Syr Richarde Ryche* from his *mooste fayethfull and humble servaunte*. Salesbury enlists Rich, himself aware of the *supersticiouse obseruaunces founded by the Byshoppe of Rome*, as his *buckeler and shylde or defence* in his attack on the *Romish Enemyes*.

There is an address to the *Christen Reader* who may be encouraged *by manifestes textes of the holye scripture* to acquiesce in the removal of *ye popish altars out of Christes Churches*. This short work, of some fifty-four pages, shows Salesbury the Protestant engaging in one of the great controversial issues of the Church of the time, debating the doctrine of the sacrifice of the

Mass as epitomized in the existence of stone altars in churches. The bishop of London, Nicholas Ridley, was prominent in the debate and Salesbury refers to him as *the victorious Metropolitane of Englande*. It is Salesbury's one real engagement in doctrinal dispute. The *botereulx* are the buttresses of the Roman Church *whyche beyng shaken downe . . . the forte wyll sone be yelded vnto my grande capitaine Jesu Christe.*

Not inappropriate to the confrontational nature of his argument is Salesbury's use of warlike metaphor from the *baterie* in the title throughout the work. Salesbury the sophister, the inheritor of medieval Scholasticism is here: the *Sic et Non* method is evident in his manner of argument. Here he is discussing the merit of the atonement of Christ pacifying the *indignacion of God. Was there anye man vpon earth able to do it? No, not one. Was there any Angel in heauen able to do it? No not one nother . . .* The Law was insufficient. As a result of Adam's fall *all mankynde halteth, hoppeth, and walloweth in the dyrty Puddle of synne.* It was the Incarnation, demonstrating the *vnspeakable mercye and the naturall kindnes* of God which *was the sole and only propiciatory sacrifice that pacified the yre of God*: for that reason altars were unnecessary in Christian churches. Salesbury addresses the Papist, *If thou wylt be content to lyue vnder the lawe of Moses, than hath Christe dyed in vayne for thee: and therefore gette the hence vnto the Jewes, whyche styll loke for a worldely Christe to come.* There is a plea for papists to be *wyllynge to renounce . . . Poperye and to receyue Christianitye.* The sanction, ultimately, is St Paul's *borde where the spirituall feaste of the Lordes Supper is celebrated vpon, the table of the Lord.* The Eucharist was the *Lordes supper, or the communion and partakynge of the bodye and bloude of Christe.*

There is a glimpse of Salesbury's upbringing as a Roman Catholic. And the work certainly displays his easy command of English which, though it is marked by the conceits and copiousness so characteristic of contemporary writing, has verve and style. Here is his account of his 'conversion': *ei droediÿarth !*

For it fared than wyth theim as it dyd wyth me, whan I was a holye Papiste, at what tyme I was at thys poynte wyth god. That if I had hearde masse boeth Sondaye and holye day, had sayde our Lady mattens, or our ladyes psalter, kissed and lycked deuoutly saintes fete (for so called thei their images) and besprynkeled my selfe well fauouredlye with coniured water, & had done the supersticious penaunce enioyned to me by my goostly, shall I saye enemye or father? Than I say was I at such poynt with God, I thought it, and assuredly beleued that I had done my full dutie vnto hym, though I neuer once called to remembraunce the benifite of Christes death, as wel in satisfiyng and pacifiynge for all the trespaces and synnes of my former euill life and naughty conuersation.

Yea . . . I thought farther that if I had done the saide vayne workes & such other no better, that I was no more beholden vnto god than he was to me, neither gaue I him more thankes for pardonyng me of my sinnes: than one marchaunt man geueth to an other for the optaynynge a peny worthe for a penie . . . And as I was thus tangeled, and abhominablye deceyued, and trayned, and brought vp in tender age, in the Popes holilyke Religion before Christes seconde byrthe here in Englande, euen so were the Iewes before hys fyrste byrthe in Iudea wonderously deceyued, and shamefully seduced and that by the fayned newe Doctryne that their Popes I meane theyr scribes and Pharises hadde brought into their churche.

Salesbury's English works are the products of his early career but an analysis of their language demonstrates his skill as a writer and his conscious craftsmanship. There is an elegance of phrase, a design of sentence and paragraph and a use of metaphor, of alliteration and other devices. He was conversant with everyday language, as expressions such as *catch who catche maye* and *sinke or swymm*e demonstrate, but he knew, too, how language could be harnessed and directed. Not only had he studied Rhetoric at university but he was to adapt and translate an important work on Rhetoric in 1552. The mechanics of language were of vital interest to William Salesbury.

VII

Two works belong to the two years following the
publication of THE BATERIE . . .; one was KYNNIVER
LLITH A BAN of 1551, a Welsh version of all the
Epistles and Gospels for the Sundays and holy days
throughout the year, Salesbury's first major contribution to presenting the Scriptures in Welsh. The other
was an adaptation and translation into Welsh of a
work on Rhetoric, TABULAE DE SCHEMATIBUS ET
TROPIS by Petrus Mosellanus. This work on Rhetoric
was not published and the original is to be found in
Cardiff Manuscript 21: the date 1552 appears in the
margin. At least nine copies were made (deriving
mainly from another copy) and this, together with
the fact that sections on Rhetoric appeared in grammar books, both published and unpublished, during
the period show that Rhetoric was regarded as a
subject of some importance. In spite of this only one
work devoted entirely to Rhetoric was actually
published in Welsh, that by Henri Perri in 1595.

Erasmus's DE DUPLICI COPIA VERBORUM AC RERUM,
compiled in 1512 at the behest of John Colet for his
pupils at St Paul's School, appeared in over a hundred editions during the sixteenth century; the
second part was concerned with various figures of
speech. When pupils and teachers needed to refer to
the classification of these figures they resorted to the
EPITOME TROPORUM AC SCHEMATUM of Joannes
Susenbrotus or the TABULAE DE SCHEMATIBUS ET
TROPIS of Petrus Mosellanus of 1529: Juan Luis Vives,
the great humanist teacher, claimed that the TABULAE
could be *hung up on the wall so that it will catch the*

attention of the pupil as he walks past it and force itself upon his eyes. This was Salesbury's source: he used it faithfully but adapted it to suit his own purpose. Mosellanus's one-sentence definition of 'Aschematiston' becomes a lengthy paragraph in Salesbury including references to the poets Guto'r Glyn and Tudur Aled.

The figures of speech were devices for adorning the literary language, devices much regarded by the humanists of western Europe. They were, of course, devices known in part to the Welsh poets and prose writers of an earlier age but by 1552 *the rhetoricians are done* (tr.) according to Salesbury and evidence suggests that training in Rhetoric had waned. Certainly it became the task of Salesbury to create a new vocabulary of rhetorical terms and to give them definition. Over a dozen new books in English appeared on Rhetoric; only one was published in Welsh, EGLVRYN PHRAETHINEB by Henri Perri in 1595, but the nine manuscript copies of Salesbury's work together with the sections devoted to Rhetoric in the Welsh grammar books of the period are indicative of the interest in the subject.

There were various definitions of the scope of Rhetoric in the sixteenth century. For Thomas Wilson in the ARTE OF RHETORIQUE (1553), it consisted of the old classical classification of Inventio, Dispositio, Elocutio, Memoria and Pronuntiatio. For Leonard Cox, ARTE OR CRAFTE OF RHETHORYKE (?1529), it included Inventio and Dispositio. For William Salesbury as for Richard Sherry in his TREATISE OF SCHEMES AND TROPES (1550), it was a matter of Elocutio and that was interpreted as figures of speech. (For Henri Perri in 1595 it consisted of

Elocutio and Pronuntiatio.) Indeed it may well have been Sherry's work which inspired Salesbury.

The treatise opens with a greeting in Welsh to Gruffudd Hiraethog *and others of his craft* (tr.). Salesbury has undertaken this task having seen Gruffudd so concerned about the condition of the language *taking upon your single shoulders too great a burden . . . collecting from here and there all kinds of tatty books to read and examine, in order to offer some sustenance towards the language which is beginning to disintegrate.* He states that he wishes to extend his *shoulder to support the same burden* and *here am I offering these figures as pillars, foundations and props to support it.* To that end, Salesbury would need the help of the poets *whom I call the architects of the language, particularly since the rhetoricians have gone.* It is not surprising, therefore, that the majority of his illustrations are taken from the Welsh poets; they demonstrate his considerable acquaintance with a variety of sources. Occasionally, he resorts to the Latin examples of Mosellanus but his main source is Welsh poetry, in contrast with the contemporary English rhetoricians who use biblical examples. Salesbury's declared purpose is to serve the poets, the details of whose craft and training remained a mystery.

His methods of creating a new set of technical rhetorical terms show him at work embellishing the language – old words assume new meanings: *diffic* in his DICTIONARY of 1547 is *Defalte* but by 1552 he endows *defic* with a technical meaning within the vocabulary of Rhetoric (*defic / eclipsis / defectus*). Compound words are created on Greek and Latin models (*kynhebycodl / homoeoptoton / similiter cadens*) and Welsh expressions are derived from the meaning of the original technical term (*kellwair du, gair sur / sarcasmus / iocus amarulentus, amara irrisio*). His method contrasts with that of the English rhetoricians who, in the main, borrow the classical forms such as eclipsis, epitrope, metaphor. Occasionally, Salesbury attempts an imaginative coining (*selsigen, bolasothach, cymysciaith / soraismus / miscella cumulatio*); for an English rhetorician, George Puttenham, in 1569 *soraismus* becomes *the mingle mangle*.

Not all Salesbury's terms, by any means, have met with the consent of the centuries though some remain in use to this day in the technical vocabulary of Rhetoric.

Salesbury's intention, as has been said, was to aid the poets. Could it be, too, that he saw in Rhetoric a further purpose? Among Cox's reasons for his compilation for his pupils at Reading Grammar School was to serve those who might become *advocates or proctors in law, or else apt to be sent as their prince's ambassadors or to be teachers of God's word . . .* The concern for God's word had become the driving force for Salesbury's energy: already, in 1551, he had demonstrated his concern with the publication of KYNNIVER LLITH A BAN.

VIII

William Salesbury had inherited the religious beliefs
of his forebears: for him and his contemporaries,
religious practice consisted of mass on Sundays and
holy days, the recitation of Our Lady's matins and
psalter and a reverence for images and being
besprynkeled . . . with coniured water. Within Wales
there seemed little dissatisfaction with such observances; murmurings of discontent and calls for reform
had been few and far between. Not that the Church
was without need of reform – the clergy, on the
whole, were ill-educated, many were absentees, the
higher clergy were seldom Welsh, and the religious
houses (once the power-houses of spirituality and
culture) were in decline. But Wales was a country of
scattered homesteads with no capital city, no university, no printing press: the mechanisms for reform
would have to come from without. The people
unquestioningly accepted the observances of the past;
they had their shrines, their altars, their images, their
pilgrimages – even their services, albeit conducted in
a language which they did not understand.

But there were changes in the air. By the time Salesbury was in his teens, the king had challenged the
authority of the pope and between 1531 and 1534
had promulgated a series of anti-papal statutes,
operable in England and Wales. The die was cast.
With the Act of Supremacy, Wales, with England,
was ushered into a new 'Church of England'. Loyalty
to the Crown ensured a great measure of obedience:
after all it was a *Tudor* crown. Although confiscation
of Church lands, the dissolution of the monasteries

and the changes in liturgy and administration were not without their hurt, the opposition to them was muted. But law was one thing: the heart was another. It was Salesbury who saw, almost earlier than anyone, that to make Protestantism work it needed to be presented in the tongue of the people of Wales.

He himself had witnessed stirrings of the heart, doubtless at Oxford; it was there that he had evidenced *Christes second byrthe*. There he had revered Erasmus; there he had heard what Luther was about. After all, Erasmus had called for reform within the Church and Luther was prepared to go further, preaching that the Christian had direct access to God and that the authority of the pope was open to question. But it was all more than opinion. The humanist respect for careful examination of texts had been directed towards Scripture: the *Versio Vulgata* which had served the Church for over a thousand years was defective – new canons of accuracy were needed and a return to the original languages of the texts of Scripture was required. In consequence, Erasmus published his Greek New Testament in 1516 with reprints in 1519, 1522, 1527 and 1535, and further editions appeared after his death. But what must have touched Salesbury, too, was that for Erasmus the translation was more than a humanistic exercise: correct rendering of Scripture was essential for a true, healthy understanding of doctrine and that demanded taking translation a step further. *I violently disagree with those who do not want to see the Scriptures in the language of the people and read by laymen*, Erasmus had declared. And Luther concurred: he produced his translation of the New Testament into German in 1522, later producing an Old Testament translation also. Luther even felt that regard for the vocabulary and idiom of the vernacular spoken word was important. The Scriptures were for the people, and lay people were assuming new roles and new power and gaining a greater degree of literacy. The printing press was at hand to serve them.

Erasmus and Luther had made their mark on Salesbury but there were others, too, one nearer home who had found talk at Oxford to his liking. William Tyndale *so skilful in seven tongues, Hebrew, Greek, Latin, Italian, Spanish, English, French* . . . as a contemporary said of him – not unlike a later remark about Salesbury – had been born *c.* 1494 in Gloucestershire, near enough to know something about Wales and the Welsh. He had embraced Protestantism and was convinced of the importance of speaking to the people, *Because I had perceived by experience, how that it was impossible to establish the lay-people in any truth, except the scripture were plainly laid before their eyes in their mother tongue, that they might see the process, order, and meaning of the text.* The day of the laity had arrived. Tyndale produced his English translation of the New Testament in 1526 and he worked abroad, preparing a new English edition of the Old Testament. But he was a man before his time and his efforts cost him his life. His English New Testament had certainly reached one Welshman who had translated parts of it before 1543.

There were others, too, who saw the need for translation. Miles Coverdale (1488–1568) produced his version of the Bible based on Tyndale's and on Latin and German editions. (It was Coverdale's third edition of A SPYRYTUALL AND MOST PRECIOUS PEARLE of 1561 which was translated as PERL MEWN ADFYD by Hugh Lewis in 1595.) In 1537 a revised edition of the Bible by Coverdale was to gain the authority of the king. Under the instruction of Thomas Cromwell, THE GREAT BIBLE of the early summer of 1539 was to be set up in every parish church; the beautiful title-page, probably the work of Hans Holbein, shows God blessing the king who, in turn, distributed copies of the Bible to Archbishop Cranmer and Thomas Cromwell. The vernacular had won.

William Salesbury was a Protestant, he was loyal to the throne and to the administration, but, above all, he was a Welshman sensible of the needs of his fellow countrymen. In that he was not alone: Sir John Price (1502-1555), an Oxford lawyer who served Cromwell, had produced in 1546 the first book to be published in Welsh, YN Y LHYVYR HWNN, containing an alphabet, a calendar, the Creed, the Lord's Prayer, the Seven Virtues of the Church and the Seven Deadly Sins together with instructions on how to read Welsh . . . and advice to farmers. In the address to the reader he remarks how *our mighty King shows no greater pleasure than to see the words of God and his gospel among his people . . . And so it is proper to put into Welsh some of the holy scripture, because there are many Welshmen who can read Welsh who cannot read one word of English or Latin* (tr.). In 1547 Salesbury expressed publicly and even more strongly than Price his hunger on behalf of his people: *Unless you wish to* *abandon, entirely, the faith of Christ . . . insist on getting the holy scripture in your language* (tr.). It was the *apologia pro sua vita*: to convert Wales to Protestantism and to do it by realizing that, to reach the minds and hearts of the Welsh people, the Scriptures and the services had to be available in Welsh.

Of course Welsh vernacular religious literature – mystical, devotional, theological, liturgical, apocryphal, *midrash*, saints' lives, short pulpit exhortations, *exempla*, biblical passages – was part of the common heritage of Christian western Europe. No one can wonder that, having made Gwynedd *glitter with limewashed churches like the firmament with stars*, as his HYSTORIA records of Gruffudd ap Cynan (1055–1137), those who attended there – and elsewhere – should have received some instruction in Welsh. Giraldus Cambrensis in his JOURNEY THROUGH WALES of 1188 refers to Archbishop Baldwin's sermons and *Alexander, Archdeacon of Bangor, acted as interpreter for the Welsh*. Indeed, Archbishop Peckham of Canterbury, scholar and reformer, in his DE INFORMATIONE SIMPLICIUM of 1281, had stated,

Let every priest in charge of a parish, four times a year, that is, once every season of the year on one solemn day or more, either in person or through another, expound to his people in the common tongue and in the simplest way the fourteen Articles of Faith, the Ten Commandments.

Peckham visited the dioceses of Wales in 1284 and there followed, in Welsh, a series of works relating to the Articles of Faith, many of them to be collected by the anchorite of Llanddewibrefi in 1346. But heresy was to halt the formal approval of the vernacular: the Ordinance of Oxford in 1407 instructed that, without licence, *no one shall in future translate on his own authority any text of holy scripture into the English tongue or into any other tongue, by way of book, booklet or treatise*. However, translations there had been, and would be; in 1546 Sir John Price referred to *the matters of Catholic faith, and the prayer which God taught us, called the pater (noster), and the ten commandments*

. . . contained in a number of old Welsh books (tr.).
Among the manuscript collections which William
Salesbury consulted – poetry and prose – were
records of earlier instruction and devotion.

Since Wales shared, with the rest of Christian
Europe, the literature of the Roman Church, even its
vernacular writing was based on the Vulgate and on
Latin compositions. Indeed, such was the sway of
Latin over the trained mind of medieval Welshmen
that most instructional manuals – scientific, medical,
grammatical, theological or religious – had their
origin in Latin writing. There may well have been
schools of translators trained in the craft of translation. One Franciscan friar, Gruffudd Bola, prefacing
his Welsh translation of the Athanasian Creed, offers
his *apologia*:

*One thing you must know at the start when one language is
translated into another as is the case of Latin into Welsh. It is
not always possible to substitute one word for another and at
the same time maintain the proper usage of the language and
adequately preserve the sense of the expression. For that reason
I have sometimes translated word for word. And other times I
have meaning for meaning, and that with sensitivity towards
the genius of our language (tr.).*

(He was grappling with the translator's dilemma of
the ages. Jerome had referred to the principle *non
verbum e verbo, sed sensum exprimere de sensu* – not a
word for a word but meaning – but Jerome was
aware, too, of the responsibility of translating *holy*
words of *holy* Scripture. The Reformation *ad fontes*
scholars and translators – Salesbury among them –
were to face the problem over and over again.)

42

But whatever existed in the collections of medieval manuscripts, one fact is certain: it was a very small amount of Scripture that had been translated into Welsh. The following comprises something of an inventory of medieval Welsh scriptural passages, listed according to source. It may well represent – at best – what material was available to Salesbury:

(a) Y BIBYL YNGHYMRAEC ('The Bible in Welsh'), belonging to the end of the thirteenth century and the beginning of the fourteenth century (with variant copies probably dating from the end of the fourteenth century existing in late sixteenth-century manuscripts, showing dependence on a Wyclif version, suggesting, interestingly, a possible Lollard influence). The title is a misnomer. It was a synopsis of the historical books of the Bible arranged genealogically and synchronistically translated mainly from the PROMPTUARIUM BIBLIAE ('Key to the Bible'), a summary by Peter of Poitiers (d. 1205) of the HISTORIA SCHOLASTICA of Peter Comestor (d. 1179). There are scriptural quotations from Genesis, biblical terms and phrases, and in addition Old Testament personal and place names given a Welsh guise. It was a popular work.

(b) GWASSANAETH MEIR ('The Office of the Blessed Virgin Mary') compiled c. 1400. Originally a monastic office it had spread in the twelfth century and the century following to the churches. The English 'Hours of the Virgin' was certainly used for private devotion and in church: there is evidence of this being the case in Welsh also. Salesbury had *sayde our Ladye mattens, or our ladyes psalter*. This included the largest number of scriptural pieces, twenty-eight psalms (Psalm XCV alone is in prose) and verses from Ecclesiastes and Luke. The psalms are based on a Vulgate translation of the psalms of the Septuagint, the Greek version of the Old Testament which was often at variance with the Hebrew original.

(c) LLYVYR AGKYR LLANDEWIVREVI ('The Book of the Anchorite of Llanddewibrefi'), copied in 1346, with several copies made later. It includes the Lord's Prayer, the Beatitudes, the 'In Principio', the Decalogue and some 150 verses from the Old and New Testaments.

(d) Y GROGLITH ('The Crucifixion') belonging to the thirteenth century possibly. There is an account of the trial and crucifixion presented in story form with the tale of the finding of the Cross. It includes a translation of Matthew 26:1–28:7. This was a popular reading for use in church.

(e) Y SEINT GREAL ('Grail' texts), belonging to the fourteenth century. This is a Welsh adaptation, abbreviated, of two French Grail texts but there is evidence, too, that the author is conversant with a text of 'Y Groglith', suggesting that the Crucifixion text had been heard over and over again as part of the Church service. This text includes some parables and verses from the New Testament. Salesbury's autograph is found in one manuscript.

This, then, was more or less the sum of the biblical diet available in Welsh at the middle of the sixteenth century. For a Renaissance scholar – and a Protestant – like William Salesbury, it was deficient: words conveyed the nuances of medieval theological thinking and nothing less than a new dependable translation of texts of Scripture was required as the

44

Three major works of Scriptural translation :
i) Kynniver Llith a Ban (1551)
ii) Llyfr Gweddi Gyffredin (1567)
iii) Testament Newydd (1567)

foundation and nurture of Christian beliefs and practice for the people of Wales. But the inheritance was a start: it made it easier for Salesbury to follow.

From Salesbury's pen came three major works of Scriptural translation: KYNNIVER LLITH A BAN (1551), LLIVER GWEDDI GYFFREDIN (1567) and TESTAMENT NEWYDD (1567). The full title of the first of these was KYNNIVER LLITH A BAN OR YSCRYTHUR LAN AC A DDARLLEIR YR ECCLEIS PRYD COMMUN Y SULIEU A'R GWILIEU TRWY'R VLWYDDYN: O CAMBEREICIAT WS ('All the lessons and articles of Holy Scripture which are read to the Church at Communion time, on the Sundays and the holy days throughout the year: the Welsh version of WS'). It appeared in 1551. It was a book of 176 pages and was *Imprinted at London by Roberte Crowley for William Salesbury dwellynge in Elye rentes in Holbourne*. Salesbury was careful to include *A copy of the Kynges moste gracious Priuilege* granted to him and John Waley in 1546 to print. It was the first major Welsh publication, in more senses than one. It is not without blemish – there are sentences missing, for example, due either to Salesbury's haste or to the fact that the typesetters were unfamiliar with Welsh. But what a pioneering achievement it was!

The work opens with a Latin address to five bishops – St David's, Llandaff, Bangor, St Asaph and Hereford (a diocese which, at that time, would have included Welsh-speakers). The letter is more than a dedication couched in terms of humanist courtesy: Salesbury issues a gentle rebuke to the bishops for their indifference to the need for the Scriptures in Welsh, and asks them to authorize his translation for use in the churches. He is content to submit his work for fair examination by six learned men from each diocese: if the translation is inadequate, he is prepared to correct it and if someone can be found to do better, so be it. In the 'dedication' he also outlines his method of translation. It is the longest continuous piece of Salesbury's Latin prose. Here is an excerpt in translation:

For a long time I had hoped to see either the people themselves, because of the love they profess towards God, or those who, by virtue of their office, have been set over them, or you their watchful Pastors to whom above all others the cure of their souls is entrusted, (I had hoped) would as suppliants beg and on their knees demand – in a word would press without yielding – that the King's Pre-eminent Majesty, Christ's vicar on earth, should consider how to uproot and destroy the extreme tyranny of the Bishop of Rome (and destroy) those bulwarks erected by foreign tongues, bulwarks . . . behind which, alas, the Word of God is bound as in fetters. But no glimpse of hope came, indeed I saw not even the slightest chance that anyone would undertake the task. Then at last, if I were to feel any mercy towards those born in the same country and nation as I – people, although ignorant of holy knowledge, who would be, without doubt, most eager of all for God . . . it seemed to me that the time was ripe . . . I translated into the British tongue the parts of the Gospels and Epistles which are read publicly . . . In St Matthew, I have mostly followed the Hebrew text, not that I dismiss the Greek, but because the Hebrew idioms seemed more akin to our own: but in all the rest I have given most heed to the Greek, preferring (as is right) to go to the fountain head than to the river.

In this 'dedication', the King has become *Christ's vicar on earth* . . . and the *Commun* (Communion) of the title-page has replaced the *mass*. Salesbury the Protestant was at work. The translation was not officially sanctioned, however, though there is evidence that it was used. Indeed in November 1561 the bishop of St Asaph was requiring *after the pistyll and gospell ys red yn Englyshe yn the churche, the same also be forthwyth there red yn Welshe aptly and distinctly* . . . A vicar of Llanasaph purchased a copy at the price of two shillings, for example.

Salesbury refers to his method of translation and the crux of his theory is a determination to return *ad fontes*. When he speaks of the Hebrew of Matthew, he is demonstrating his awareness of the fact that this Gospel contains much quotation from the Old Testament and for this reason he would consult the Hebrew text. (In Matthew 1:23 he even reproduces 'Emmanuel' as 'Nghimanwel', attempting to convey the Hebrew form and the wording of Isaiah 7:14). When he speaks of his preference for the fountain head to the river, the allusion is to the greater authority of the Hebrew or Greek original over the many contemporary translations and editions. The 'dedication' presents his methodology for Scriptural translation.

What, then, were Salesbury's sources? The Act of Uniformity had enforced the use of the BOOK OF COMMON PRAYER of 1549 in all churches. This was the basis of Salesbury's translation. It had included the Epistles and Gospels from the GREAT BIBLE of 1539. But a straightforward translation from that translation was not enough to satisfy Salesbury. He wanted to use the new sources available and to provide what he regarded as an accurate translation. His consultations must have included, in addition to the BOOK OF COMMON PRAYER of 1549, which included seven pieces taken from the Old Testament, and the GREAT BIBLE of 1539, the Latin translation of the Hebrew Bible prepared by Sebastian Münster in

1535, which included the Hebrew version. There was Erasmus's New Testament of 1535, containing his Greek text, his Latin translation and notes; also Erasmus's translation of 1527 which included the Vulgate. Then there were the editions of Luther, Tyndale and Coverdale. (Indeed Salesbury's 'dedication' to the bishops is reminiscent of Tyndale's remarks in his introductions.) In the wording of his own translation there is sometimes a feeling that Salesbury is struggling to produce the most appropriate word or phrase: there is a choice, a rejection, an acceptance. The glosses in the margin (*the pestylent gloses* as Henry VIII describes Tyndale's insertions) are part of the struggle. As if it were a mathematical exercise, Salesbury shows his 'workings', for his own purpose and for the reader. Because, like Luther and Tyndale, he recognized that he was composing with an end in view – to make the Bible understood by the laity. Whatever his consultations, above all else was his feeling for Welsh idiom, syntax, vocabulary, which his researches into earlier literature had provided: not only would the phrases of the earlier Welsh versions of the Office of the Blessed Virgin Mary and the Crucifixion be incorporated but also the vocabulary and idiom which he had collected from various sources. At the same time he was conscious of the standing of Scripture and the necessity of preserving its dignity, which is why he was at pains to give a Latin appearance to some of his words.

It has been said that his translation of the epistles is not as good as his gospel translations: there was unease at his quirks of orthography and word derivation. But as a first draft, so to speak, the work

48

is truly remarkable. Here is an excerpt from the Epistle for the Tuesday before Easter (taken from Isaiah 50); it is followed by the rendering in the BOOK OF COMMON PRAYER of 1549:

Yr Arglwyð ðeo a egores vycclust / a myvy ny wrthodeis / ac nyd enkiliais im gwrthgarn. Vyccorph a ðodeis y rei ae maeðei am gruðieu y rei ae tamigei: am wynep ny chuðieis rac mynych warth / na rac poeri arno. Am Arglwyð ðeo am kymorth: am hynny nim gwradwiðir: ac o bleit hyn y caledeis vy wynep val y mayn callestr / a mi wn na'm gwradwyðir. Yn gyuagos y may hwn am cyfiownai: Pwy a ymdatle a myfy? Safwn ynghyt: od edldy nep yn vy erbyn? dawet attaf vi. Nycha yr Arglwyð ðeo am kymorth i: Pwy velly am beirn? Nycha wyntwy oll a henant mal [gwisc] / ar pryf ae yssa wy . . . [dillat neca dach]

The Lorde God hath opened myne eare, therfore can I not saye naye, neither withdrawe myselfe: but I offre my backe unto the smiters, and my chekes to the nyppers: I turne not my face from shame and spittyng, and the Lorde God shall helpe me, therfore shall I not bee confounded. I haue hardened my face lyke a flynte stone, for I am sure that I shall not come to confusion. He is at hande that iustifyeth me, who will then go to lawe with me? Let us stande one against another; yf there be any that will reason with me, lette hym come here forth unto me. Beholde the Lorde God standeth by me, what is he then that can condemne me? loe, they shall bee all lyke as an olde clothe, the mothe shall eate them up . . .

Within two years of the publication of KYNNIVER LLITH A BAN, the course of Protestantism was officially halted with the accession to the throne of the Catholic Mary. There would be a return to old liturgies, to Latin and to old observances. Salesbury withdrew and must have lived quietly – maybe in Llansannan – for the next five years, reading, hopefully preparing for his great mission. His chance was to come with Mary's death and the succession of the

49

Protestant Elizabeth. Richard Davies, some fifteen years older than Salesbury, was one who had fled during Mary's reign: like Salesbury he was an Oxford man from Denbighshire who shared the same sense of Welsh culture. During his exile Davies had lived in Frankfurt among a group of Protestants: he may well have visited Geneva where John Calvin was writing his commentaries and where Theodore Beza, friend of and successor to Calvin, was working on a new edition of the Greek New Testament. Beza had published a new Latin translation in 1556. And in the buzz of all the Protestant scriptural and theological activity there were those who saw the opportunity of preparing versions in their own vernaculars. From such diligence there emanated a new English version derived from Hebrew and Greek texts, ready to rekindle Protestant lights: the result was a New Testament of 1557 and a Bible of 1560, both published in Geneva. The former was the work of William Whittingham and the Bible of 1560 was based on the work of Tyndale and the Great Bible but was also influenced by Calvin, Beza and the French Bibles of Lefèvre and Olivetan. This 1560 Bible was the first English edition to use numbered verses. In it the address to the reader, 'To ovr Beloved in the Lord', makes its authors' point:

. . . we thoght that we colde bestowe our labours & studie in nothing which colde be more acceptable to God and comfortable to his Churche then in the translating of the holy Scriptures into our natiue tongue: the which thing, albeit that diuers hertofore haue indououred to atchieue: yet considering the infancie of those tymes and imperfect knollage of the tongues, in respect of this ripe age and cleare light which God hath now reueiled, the translations required greatly to be perused and reformed . . .

Richard Davies could not have witnessed such activity and thinking without recalling Salesbury's attempts and when he returned as bishop to St Asaph early in 1560 the opportunity came to discuss Welsh versions of the Scriptures further. There, too, Davies found other kindred spirits, devoted to scholarship and literature, men like Gruffudd Hiraethog . . . and, of course, Salesbury himself. Was it Davies who kindled new energy in Salesbury? It may well have been so and that it was Salesbury who was author of the 'Appeal' – a copy of which was among Richard Davies's papers – made to members of the Privy Council in 1561:

. . . to provide . . . either by serchyng sendyng & callyng for the godlyest & best learned men in diuinitee or knowledge of ye holy Scriptures of the walsh tong wt all . . . may consult together what way be thought most expedient, & what remedie most present for the expulsment of sooch miserable darknes for the lack of the shynyng lyght of Christe's Gospell as yet styll remayneth among the inhabitantes of the same principalitie . . . that then it may please your good lordships to wyll and require and com'aund the learned men to traducte the boke of the Lordes Testament into the vulgare walsh tong . . .

But such a provision would call for authorization. Richard Davies as a member of the House of Lords was crucial in obtaining this, and Humphrey Lhuyd, known to both Davies and Salesbury and one of the three to whom Salesbury had dedicated OLL SYNN-WYR PEN, member of Parliament for Denbigh, was the key man in the Commons. Without doubt it was due to their influence and resolve that the Act of 1563 was passed by which the bishops of Wales and Hereford were ordered to ensure *That the whole Bible, containing the New Testament and the Old, with the Book of the Common Prayer and Administration of the Sacraments, as is now used within this Realm in English, to be truly and exactly translated,* as a modern rescension has it, adding the part that determined that there should be an English version, too, in all churches so that the laity *by conferring both Tongues together, the sooner attain to the Knowledge of the English Tongue.* This was to come into effect by 1 March 1567; but, in the mean time, Welsh was to be the language of services in the Welsh-speaking parts, and the Epistles and Gospels were to be read at every Communion service. (Already the Litany had been translated in 1562 but no copy remains.) There was no delaying Salesbury: in 1563, in the company of John Waley the publisher, he was to apply for a licence to print the Bible and Prayer Book for a period of seven years. (In the event the licence was not used.)

Richard Davies became bishop of St David's in 1561; Salesbury stayed at the bishop's palace at Abergwili between 1564 and 1566 and then went to London to oversee the Prayer Book and the New Testament through the press. Already Davies had been engaged in translating the books of Joshua, Judges, Ruth and I and II Samuel into English for the new English version of 1568; in a letter to Archbishop Parker, Davies remarks, *I am in hande to performe yo'r requeste and wyll vse as moche diligens and spede as I can hauyng smale helpe for that or for the welshe Bible. Mr Salusbury onely taketh paen w'th me.* In 1565 Beza's *magnum opus* on the New Testament was published: it contained the Greek text, a Latin translation and the Vulgate together with copious notes. The bishop and Salesbury must have studied it with *moche diligens* and perhaps examined others of the many renderings which were appearing, some more concerned with

Renaissance Latin style than they were with exactness.

ii) The Welsh Prayer Book, LLIVER GWEDDI GYFFREDIN ('The Book of Common Prayer') carried, on its title-page, a consent *Vewed, perused and allowed by the Bishops, accordyng to the Act stablished for the translation of the Bible and thys Booke into the Brytyshe tongue. Imprinted at London by Henry Denham, at the costes and charges of Humfrey Toy. Anno. 1567. 6. Maij. Cum Priuilegio.* The original intention was to publish the Psalter separately but it appeared with the rest of the book.

Basically it reproduced the BOOK OF COMMON PRAYER in its revised form of 1564. There is nothing to say that Salesbury was the translator though textual analysis gives incontrovertible evidence of his work. It is a major achievement. Revision was not something Salesbury shunned. Scholarship had advanced since 1551 and he had gained experience. By now the Geneva Bible of 1560 (and its New Testament of 1557) had appeared as had the Beza of 1556, apart from the earlier works, the GREAT BIBLE, Coverdale, Tyndale, Luther, Erasmus, the Vulgate, earlier Welsh translations and his own previous efforts. This time Beza and Geneva were to be at his right hand, reminding him that total accuracy was all-important: anything added for the sake of clarity, Salesbury would put into brackets. But often Salesbury was to be his own man – selecting, rejecting, translating for himself.

What of the qualities of LLIVER GWEDDI GYFFREDIN? It displays much the same basic characteristics as KYNNIVER LLITH A BAN though the orthographic quirks are slightly fewer. Fewer, too, are the recent English borrowings. Again there are Latinized forms, bolstering the dignity and pedigree of Welsh, and here too, on occasion, he uses more than one translation to demonstrate the copiousness of the language. There are old words and phrases and new creations. In some instances he has lost the bounce of the translations in KYNNIVER LLITH A BAN, but accuracy, now, could not be sacrificed. All in all it is a work of extraordinary merit, matching scholarship with poetry. Here is an excerpt from the Gospel for St Mark's Day – from John 15 – taken from the LLIVER GWEDDI, followed by the same passage from the Geneva New Testament of 1557:

MI ywr wir winwyδen, a'm Tat ys y ¹lavurwr. Pop caingen ny ddwc ffrwyth ynofi, ef ei tynn ymaith: a' phop vn a ddwc ffrwyth, ef ei ²carth, mal hi dyco mwy o ffrwyth, Yr awrhon ydd ywch' yn lan can y gair, a ddywedais ychwi. Aroswch ynof, a mi ynoch: megis na 'al' y gaingen δwyn ffrwyth o hanei ehun, anyd erys yn y winwydden, velly nyd ellwch chwi, anyd aroswch ynof. Mi yw'r winwydden: chwi yw'r cangenae: Y nep a aroso ynof, a mi yndaw, hwnn a ddwc ffrwyth lawer: can ys eb ofi, ny ellwch 'wneythy dim. An'd erys vn ynofi, e a ³tav lwyt allan val cangen, ac a ⁴wywa: ac y cesclir wy ac ei tavlir yn tan, ac ei lloscir. A'd aroswch ynof, ac aros o'm gairiae ynoch, erchwch beth bynac a ewyllysoch, ac eu gwnair ychwy . . . Mal y carawδ Tat vi, velly y cerais i chwi: trigwch yn vygcariat . . .

¹diwylliawdr tir   ²glanha   ³vwrir   ⁴grina

I AM the true vine, and my Father is an housband man. Euery branche that beareth not frute in me, he taketh away: and euery branche that beareth frute, he pourgeth, that it may bring forth more frute. Now are ye cleane through the wordes which I haue spoken vnto you. Bide in me, and I in you. as the branche can not beare frute of it selfe, except it abyde in the vine: no more can ye, except ye abyde in me. I am the vine, ye are the branches. he that abydeth in me, and I in him, the same bringeth forthe muche frute. For without me, can ye do nothing. If a man byde not in me, he is cast forthe as a branche, and withereth: and men gather them and cast them into the fyre, and they burne. If ye byde in me and my wordes also in you: aske what ye wyl, and it shalbe done to you . . . As my Father hath loued me, even so haue I loued you: Continue in my loue . . .

Within six months of the publication of the Welsh BOOK OF COMMON PRAYER there appeared the Welsh translation of the New Testament, TESTAMENT NEW-YDD EIN ARGLWYDD IESV CHRIST. It was published on 7 October 1567, printed by *Henry Denham, at the costes and charges of Humfrey Toy, dwelling in Paules church yarde, at the signe of the Helmet.* It was a volume of 426 pages. The title-page in Welsh reads:

The New Testament of our Lord Jesus Christ drawn, as far as the different idiom allowed, word for word from the Greek and Latin, changing the form of the letters of the inserted words. Beside this each word deemed to be unintelligible, either because of the local dialect, or because of the unfamiliarity of the matter, has been noted and explained on the margin of the same page (tr.).

There are three contributors to the translation noted in the text: Richard Davies, bishop of St David's (1 Timothy, Hebrews, Epistle of James, I and II Peter), Thomas Huet, precentor of St David's *(all the text of the Apocalypsis into his own dialect* (tr.) – he was the one south Walian, whose usages include *whilio* 'search', *doyddeg* 'twelve', *hoyl* 'sun') and Salesbury (all the rest including the translation from the Geneva Bible of the 'arguments' and the 'contents', with the exception of the Epistle of James). Much of the translation, therefore, is Salesbury's and he, clearly, is also 'editor'.

Richard Davies's other contribution was his EPISTLE TO THE WELSH (tr.), the *apologia* for Welsh Protestantism, explaining how the pristine form of Christianity among the Welsh had been corrupted by Rome. It was a theory much in vogue and it fitted in well – at a time of Welsh ascendancy through their Tudor monarchs – with the desire for acceptability of Protestantism. Perhaps Salesbury had a hand in the epistle: certainly he echoes the sentiments in his own EPISTLE TO THE WELSH:

TO ALL THE WELSH PEOPLE who love the faith of their forebears the old British . . .

Just as metalworkers have a proverb that the best gold is the old gold, and as those who treat of the history of the people of the world would say that the best companion is the old one: so also those who diligently delve into Holy Scripture say that the best faith is the old faith . . . And for this (reason) woe betide the one who calls this a new faith, whether he do so in ignorance or through cunning, to deceive himself and to mislead the people. It is to this faith, in his above Epistle that the honourable Father D.R.D. second St David of Menevia seeks to invite you, to guide you and to lead you for your soul's sake. It is not right that after him, least of all one so frail of learning as myself, should say anything upon the matter of which he has treated . . .(tr.).

There is also a 'dedication' to the Queen, written by Salesbury in the style of Renaissance dedications:

I can not, most Christian Prince, and gracious Soueraine, but euen as dyd the poore blynde Bartimeus, or Samaritane lepre to our Sauior, so com I before your maiesties feete, and there lying prostrate not onely for my self, but also for the deliuery of many thousands of my countrey folkes from the spirituall blyndnes of ignoraunce, and fowl infection of olde Idolatrie and false superstition, most humbly, and dutifully to acknowlege your incomparable benefite bestowed vpon vs in graunting the sacred Scriptures the verye remedie & salue of our gostly blyndnes and leprosie, to be had in our best knowen tongue.

There had been little time for revision of the work done for his LLIVER GWEDDI though there are instances of Salesbury's struggling yet again for a better and more correct translation. When he was working on his New Testament he would have kept at his side his own work on the Book of Common Prayer, his earlier attempts together with – undoubtedly – Robert Estienne's Greek text of the New Testament in 1550, Beza's Latin version of 1556 and the New Testament and Bible of Geneva, 1557 and 1560. The earlier influence of Erasmus, the Vulgate, Luther, Tyndale, the GREAT BIBLE and Coverdale is less marked. But, after all, there had been new scholarship and a new insistence on accuracy. And when Salesbury disagreed with any version, he made his own way. He was determined to make use of everything that was available, but again his ear for Welsh and his knowledge of it in its literary manifestations were always there.

The characteristics of his writing remain – little English-language influence, old words, new creations (modelled element by element), occasional borrowing, Latinization for the purpose of marking the prestige of Welsh and attempts to prove the copiousness of the Welsh vocabulary. Sometimes he offered too much choice in his text, the expression is marred by his philological and orthographic theories. But overall is his literary touch. Richard Davies had referred to the rendering as *translated into Welsh faithfully, correctly, through care and perseverance* (tr.). He might have added, *and with flair.* It stands well beside the other contemporary vernacular translations of Scripture and, as far as accuracy was concerned, was unsurpassed.

Here is an excerpt from St Mark's Gospel 4 followed by the English of the Geneva Version of 1557:

AC ef a ddechreawdd drachefyn precethy yn-glan y mor, a' thyrfa vawr a ymglascawdd ataw, yn yd aeth ef y long, ac eistedd yn y mor, a'r oll popul oedd ar y tir wrth y mor. Ac ef a ddyscawdd yddwynt laweredd ¹ym-parabolae, ac a ddyvot wrthwynt yn y ddysc ef. Gwrandewch: Nycha, ydd aeth heywr allan y heheu. Ac e ddarvu val ydd oedd ef yn heheu, cwympo o ²beth wrth vin y ffordd, ac a ddaeth ehediait ³y nef ac ei ⁴difasont. A' pheth a gwympodd ar dir caregawc, lle nid oedd iddo vawr ddaiar, ac yn y van yr eginawdd, can nad oedd iddo ddyfnder daiar. A' phan godaw haul, y ⁵gwresogwyt ef, a' chan nad oedd ynddo wreiddyn, y tra gwywawdd. A' pheth a gwympiawdd ymplith ⁶y drain a'r drain a dyfeson ac ei tageson, val na roddes ffrwyth. A' pheth arall a gwympiodd mewn tir da, ac a roddes ffrwyth ac a eginawdd i vynydd, ac a dyfawdd, ac a dduc, peth ar ei ddecfed ar vgain, peth ar ei drugainvet, a' pheth ar ei ganvet. Yno y dyvot ef wrthwynt, Y nep 'sy ganthaw glustiae i wrandaw, gwrandawet . . .

¹ar ddameg-ion, cyffelyp-wraethae   ²vn, rei   ³yr awyr ⁴bwyteson, ysyson   ⁵diwrydywyt yr   ⁶yr yscall

AND he began agayn to teache by the sea side, and ther gathered vnto him much people, insomuch, that he entred into a shyp, and sate in the sea, and all the people was by the sea syde on the shore. And he taught them many thynges in similitudes, and sayd vnto them in his doctrine. Hearken to, Beholde, there went out a sower to sowe. And it fortuned as he sowed, that some fel by the way syde, and the fowles of the ayre came and deuoured it vp. Some fel on stony grounde, where it had not much earth: and by and by sprang vp, because it had not depth of earth. But as sone as the sunne was vp, it caught heate, and because it had not rootyng, wythered away. And some fel among the thornes, and the thornes grewe vp and choked it, so that it gaue no frute. And some fel in good grounde, and dyd yelde frute that sprong and grew, and broght forth, some thyrty folde, some syxty folde, and some an hundred folde. And he sayd vnto them, He that hath eares to heare, let him heare . . .

IX

According to Sir John Wynn of Gwydir, Richard
Davies and Salesbury were collaborating on an
edition of the Old Testament with the aim of producing the whole Bible in Welsh but they disagreed
over the use of one word. Be that as it may, work on
the Old Testament did not proceed but Salesbury
continued to copy manuscripts and to annotate
others and in good Renaissance fashion turned his
hand to yet another area of humanistic interest. This
was his LLYSIEULYFR MEDDYGINIAETHOL, 'Medicinal
Herbal', which belongs to the period 1568–1574. The
original manuscript is lost but a copy was made by
Roger Morris of Coed-y-talwrn in 1597. Morris was
a distinguished copyist: he claimed to have borrowed
the original from Thomas Wiliems who referred to
Salesbury in 1574 as 'phisicwr godidoc', a splendid
physician/mediciner.

As elsewhere, there were herbals in medieval Wales,
not surprisingly remembering the place of honour
accorded to the mediciner in the Welsh laws. Among
the best known of the medical treatises is the one
associated with the Physicians of Myddfai, a copy of
which is found in the Red Book of Hergest (c. 1382–
1410). Another important collection, written c. 1400,
now Havod Manuscript 16, contains herbals, the
names of herbs, the vapours and the properties of
herbs. Two further interesting manuscripts are Jesus
7, dating from the fifteenth century, which contains
parts of the material from the Physicians of Myddfai,
a medical treatise and a calendar, and Llanstephan 10

written by David ap Griffith, priest, in 1515 and including herbals, a Latin–Welsh list of names of herbs and a study of the vapours. In addition, Gutun Owain, the poet and genealogist, had transcribed some medical texts and drawings during the year 1488–9.

The rediscovery of the ancient world and the advent of printing gave a new impetus to the study of botanical and medical works. The writings of Hippocrates, Galen, Dioscorides and Pliny were the exemplars. Scholars in Italy, France, Germany and England published works which described plants possessing medicinal qualities and it is of significance that some 400,000 copies of medical works appeared in English from the press between 1486 and 1604. Nothing was published in Welsh though Welshmen were engaged in writing, like Humphrey Lloyd of Leighton (fl. 1497–1554), translator of two popular works, THE TREASURY OF HEALTH (1552) and THE JUDGEMENT OF URINES (1553). The former work was translated into Welsh by Jhon ap Ifan (British Museum MS 15078) in 1585. Others were Robert Recorde of Tenby (?1510–1558), author of THE VRINAL OF PHYSICK and Thomas Phaer of Cilgerran (?1510–1560), author of BOOK OF CHILDREN, the 1544 edition of which concludes with 'Thus endeth the book of children composed by Thomas Phayer, studiouse in medicine . . .' This work was translated into Welsh by Elis Gruffydd, the soldier of Calais who also translated Phaer's adaptation, REGIMENT OF LIFE (as he did Sir Thomas Elyot's THE CASTEL OF HELTH which appeared in sixteen editions between 1536 and 1595). All these translations by Elis Gruffydd are to be found in Cwrtmawr MS 1. The subject of medicine appealed greatly to Elis Gruffydd who said of it: *this art is the greatest remedy which the Father from heaven has ordained* (tr.).

Salesbury would have been conversant with these publications, though it may be that contemporary criticism of his work (the *wordes being quareled withall* in 1567) or of his orthography in particular prevented him from taking his LLYSIEULYFR eventually to press: perhaps it was that by that time his financial support was lacking, too, and the market might have been uncertain. The LLYSIEULYFR is basically a paraphrase of some of the best-known herbals of the sixteenth century, in particular the DE HISTORIA STIRPIUM by Leonhard Fuchs/Fuchsius (whom Salesbury described as *the chief botanist of our age* (tr.)) which first appeared in 1542 with full-page woodcuts. Another source for Salesbury was William Turner's A NEW HERBALL, WHEREIN ARE CONTEYNED THE NAMES OF HERBES . . . WITH THE PROPERTIES DEGRES AND NATURALL PLACES OF THE SAME, a complete edition of which appeared in 1568. Both works were much indebted to the classical exemplars to which reference has already been made.

It is not easy to estimate fully the qualities of the LLYSIEULYFR since Salesbury's original is not available. Certainly, there are signs of a first draft – sometimes unidiomatic Welsh follows a hurried word-for-word translation. But the Welsh very often has verve and charm. There is reference to Salesbury's Wales – *alisma, palantan y Dwfr* grows in plenty *on the edge of the lake which is about the main residence of Sir John Salisbury Knight* (tr.), and there are references to Lleweni and Denbigh (and the houses of Huw Dryhurst and Robert Huxley). Radish was to be found *growing in a garden called the priests' garden near the city of Tübingen in Germany and in the garden of the monks to the west of the monastery of Aberconway . . . and from there I moved it to my garden* (tr.).

The entries normally follow the same pattern – the name(s) in Latin, English, Welsh, a description, where to find them, what season of the year and what properties they possess. Here is a short excerpt from *Suran y gog*:

Oxis in Greek and Latin, allelu then cockowes meate, or Wood sorel in English and suran y gog in Welsh . . . three small leaves . . . among trees and damp craggy places . . . in April and sometimes in May that is the first hearing of the cuckoo . . . good for weak stomach . . . and sores of the mouth. (tr.)

There is a personal reflection, too:

Fuchsius says and others who proved it right that when these herbs grow thick and ample there will be much rain and water-flow that year and when the flowers on them are few, it signifies dry weather. And I myself saw that to be true of the dampness of the year 1555 . . .(tr.)

The year 1555 had seen Salesbury kept indoors for other reasons than weather conditions but his recall shows something of his mind. He observed and he recorded. The LLYSIEULYFR was to be his last work. In 1574, Thomas Wiliems said of him, *we shall yet have (if God sees fit to grant him life) many notable pieces of his work* (tr.). It was not to be so.

X

Not all among his contemporaries nor those who
came later looked on his labours with admiration. It
is true that his theories and quirks of language and
orthography did not help his reputation and there
were occasions when he used vocabulary which was
far beyond the understanding of his intended audience: his alternative readings, on occasion, created
confusion rather than clarity. But in some of these
matters he must be measured within the context of
his time. Orthography was a subject of concern, and
variety of words and expressions was regarded as a
strength: *copie*, copiousness, was a quality much
regarded by his English contemporaries and *molta
copiosa* was an Italian remark of admiration. Above
all Salesbury remains the outstanding example of the
Welsh Renaissance scholar, broad in his range and
interests (language, law, theology, history, science,
literature, medicine), inquisitive and enquiring, who
believed that to prosper culturally Wales had to
become part of the new Europe: he wished to see the
learning of the Renaissance and all its conceits, *tutti
concetti*, within the grasp of his fellow countrymen.
Not only was he convinced that Protestantism was
worth promoting but he was prepared to devote his
energies and his talents to providing the means by
which his countrymen *shoulde participate and enjoy the
incomparable treasure of Christes Euangelie* as it had
been enjoyed in its purity long, long ago.

His scholarship was considerable and his output
immense. It has been said recently that Luther

translated the entire New Testament in a matter of weeks into fine German, powerful and warm: he not only made it the dominant influence in German religion, but creatively shaped the modern German language. Salesbury deserves similar praise, certainly in part. But perhaps his greatest contribution was that, grounded as he was in the indigenous literature of Wales, he was able to create a vibrant medium by grafting new vocabulary and new forms of expression onto the richness of the language which he inherited. It was his genius for matching the new with the old that was his outstanding achievement. It was his background, his ear, his talent and taste for words which made him capable of writing extremely fine prose as Bishop Morgan recognized. After all, Morgan virtually adopted Salesbury's New Testament into his Bible of 1588. There could hardly have been a greater tribute than that. Wales had no court, no university, no academy, no salon, as other countries had, to give its language sanction. In the case of Wales, the Bible of 1588 became the canon of *bel usage*. Salesbury played no small part in preparing the way for it.

A Select Bibliography

THE WORKS OF WILLIAM SALESBURY

A DICTIONARY IN ENGLYSHE AND WELSHE, 1547. A Scolar Press Facsimile, Menston, 1969.

OLL SYNNWYR PEN KEMBERO YGYD, 1547. Edited by J. Gwenogvryn Evans, Bangor and London, 1902.

A BRIEFE AND A PLAYNE INTRODUCTION, 1550. A Scolar Press Facsimile, Menston, 1968.

THE DESCRIPCION OF THE SPHERE OR FRAME OF THE WORLDE, 1550.

BAN WEDY I DYNNY . . ., 1550. Edited by J. H. Davies. Published with YNY LHYVYR HWNN, Bangor and London, 1902.

THE BATERIE OF THE POPES BOTEREULX, 1550.

KYNNIVER LLITH A BAN . . .,1551. Edited by John Fisher, Cardiff and Oxford, 1931.

'Llyfr Rhetoreg', 1552. Cardiff MS 21.

LLIVER GWEDDI GYFFREDIN, 1567. Facsimile, with introduction by Melville Richards and Glanmor Williams, Cardiff, 1965.

TESTAMENT NEWYDD, 1567. Reprint, edited by ?Isaac Jones, Caernarfon, 1850 (A faithful reprint, up to

Revelation XVIII; thereafter several errors). Excerpts with Introduction by Thomas Parry, DETHOLION O DESTAMENT NEWYDD 1567, Cardiff, 1967.

A PLAYNE AND A FAMILIAR INTRODUCTION . . ., 1567.

'Llysieulyfr Meddyginiaethol', 1568–1574. The original copy no longer exists: National Library of Wales MS 4581 is the copy made by Roger Morris. An imperfect copy was made later by Evan Thomas, now National Library of Wales MS 686: it was this copy that was edited by E. Stanton Roberts, Liverpool, 1916.

WORKS OF REFERENCE

 J. Atkinson, 'Martin Luther' in Sinclair B. Ferguson and David F. Wright (eds.), THE NEW DICTIONARY OF THEOLOGY, Leicester, 1988.

D. J. Bowen, GRUFFUDD HIRAETHOG A'I OES, Cardiff, 1958.

I. Bowen, THE STATUTES OF WALES, London, 1908.

John Cule, 'The Court Mediciner and Medicine in the Laws of Wales', JOURNAL OF THE HISTORY OF MEDICINE, Volume XXI, 1966.

John Cule, 'Medical Translations in Sixteenth Century Wales', XXVII International Congress of the History of Medicine, Barcelona, 1980.

Ceri Davies, RHAGYMADRODDION A CHYFLWYNIADAU LLADIN 1551–1632, Cardiff, 1980.

Ceri Davies, LATIN WRITERS OF THE RENAISSANCE, Cardiff, 1981.

THE ENGLISH HEXAPLA, London, 1841.

D. Simon Evans, MEDIEVAL RELIGIOUS LITERATURE, Cardiff, 1986.

I. Foster, 'The Book of the Anchorite', British Academy, 1950.

Clara Gebert (ed.), AN ANTHOLOGY OF ELIZABETHAN DEDICATIONS AND PREFACES, Pennsylvania, 1933.

E. C. S. Gibson, THE FIRST AND SECOND PRAYER BOOK OF EDWARD VI, London, 1957.

R. G. Gruffydd, 'The Welsh Book of Common Prayer', JOURNAL OF THE HISTORICAL SOCIETY OF THE CHURCH IN WALES, XVII, 1967.

R. G. Gruffydd, 'Humphrey Llwyd: Dyneiddiwr', EFRYDIAU ATHRONYDDOL, XXXIII, 1970.

R. G. Gruffydd, Y BEIBL A DROES I'W BOBL DRAW: THE TRANSLATION OF THE BIBLE INTO THE WELSH TONGUE, Cardiff, 1988.

Heledd Hayes, CYMRU A'R DADENI, Y Colegiwm Cymraeg, 1987.

Trevor Herbert and Gareth Elwyn Jones (eds.), TUDOR WALES, Cardiff, 1988.

Garfield Hughes, RHAGYMADRODDION 1547–1659, Cardiff, 1976.

J. Isaacs, 'The Sixteenth Century Versions', in H. Wheeler Robinson (ed.), THE BIBLE IN ITS ANCIENT AND ENGLISH VERSIONS, Oxford, 1940.

Richard Foster Jones, THE TRIUMPH OF THE ENGLISH LANGUAGE, Stanford, 1953.

R. Brinley Jones, THE OLD BRITISH TONGUE: THE VERNACULAR IN WALES 1540–1640, Cardiff, 1970.

R. Brinley Jones, 'Yr Iaith sydd yn kychwyn ar Dramgwydd', YSGRIFAU BEIRNIADOL VIII, Denbigh, 1974.

R. Brinley Jones, 'Geirfa Rhethreg 1552–1632', YSGRIFAU BEIRNIADOL IX, Denbigh, 1976.

Thomas Jones (ed.), Y BIBYL YNGHYMRAEC, Cardiff, 1940.

Thomas Jones, 'Pre-Reformation Welsh Versions of the Scriptures', NATIONAL LIBRARY OF WALES JOURNAL, IV, 1946.

Henry Lewis, 'Darnau o'r Efengylau', Y CYMMRODOR XXXI, 1921.

Saunders Lewis, 'Damcaniaeth Eglwysig Brotestannaidd', EFRYDIAU CATHOLIG ii, 1947.

W. Alun Mathias, 'Astudiaeth o Weithgarwch Llenyddol William Salesbury', MA thesis, University of Wales, Cardiff, 1949.

W. Alun Mathias, 'Llyfr Rhetoreg William Salesbury', LLÊN CYMRU I, 1951.

W. Alun Mathias, 'William Salesbury — Ei Fywyd a'i Weithiau', in Geraint Bowen (ed.), Y TRADDODIAD RHYDDIAITH, Llandysul, 1970.

W. Alun Mathias, 'William Salesbury — Ei Ryddiaith', in Geraint Bowen (ed.), Y TRADDODIAD RHYDD-IAITH, Llandysul, 1970.

Morfydd E. Owen, 'Meddygon Myddfai: A Preliminary Survey of some Medieval Medical Writing in Welsh', STUDIA CELTICA X–XI, 1975/6.

Morfydd E. Owen, 'Functional Prose: Religion, Science, Grammar, Law', in A. O. H. Jarman and Gwilym Rees Hughes (eds.), A GUIDE TO WELSH LITERATURE Volume I, Swansea, 1976.

Prys Morgan, A BIBLE FOR WALES, 1988.

Brynley F. Roberts (ed.), GWASSANAETH MEIR, Cardiff, 1961.

De Witt T. Starnes and Gertrude E. Noyes, THE ENGLISH DICTIONARY FROM CAWDREY TO JOHNSON, 1604–1755, Chapel Hill, 1946.

D. R. Thomas, THE LIFE AND WORK OF BISHOP DAVIES AND WILLIAM SALESBURY, Oswestry, 1902.

Isaac Thomas, WILLIAM SALESBURY AND HIS TESTAMENT, Cardiff, 1967.

Isaac Thomas, Y Testament Newydd Cymraeg 1551–1620, Cardiff, 1976.

Isaac Thomas, Yr Hen Destament Cymraeg 1551–1620, Aberystwyth, 1988.

S. Minwel Tibbott (ed.), Castell yr Iechyd gan Elis Gruffydd, Cardiff, 1969.

Glanmor Williams, 'William Salesbury's *Baterie of the Pope's Botereulx*', Bulletin of the Board of Celtic Studies XIII iii, 1949.

Glanmor Williams, Bywyd ac Amserau'r Esgob Richard Davies, Cardiff, 1953.

Glanmor Williams, The Welsh Church from Conquest to Reformation, Cardiff, 1962, 1976.

Glanmor Williams, Welsh Reformation Essays, Cardiff, 1967.

Glanmor Williams, Religion, Language and Nationality, Cardiff, 1979.

Glanmor Williams, 'Religion and Welsh Literature in the Age of the Reformation', British Academy, London/Oxford, 1983.

Glanmor Williams, Recovery, Reorientation and Reformation in Wales c. 1415–1642, Oxford, Cardiff, 1987.

Glanmor Williams, The Reformation in Wales, Bangor, 1991.

J. E. Caerwyn Williams, 'Rhyddiaith Grefyddol Cymraeg Canol', Y TRAETHODYDD, XCVII, 1942.

J. E. Caerwyn Williams, 'Medieval Welsh Religious Prose', PROCEEDINGS OF THE INTERNATIONAL CON-GRESS OF CELTIC STUDIES, Cardiff, 1963.

J. E. Caerwyn Williams, 'Rhyddiaith yn yr Oesau Canol', in Geraint Bowen (ed.), Y TRADDODIAD RHYDDIAITH YN YR OESAU CANOL, Llandysul, 1974.

J. E. Caerwyn Williams, GEIRIADURWYR Y GYMRAEG YNG NGHYFNOD Y DADENI, Amgueddfa Werin Cymru, 1983.

G. J. Williams, 'Traddodiad Llenyddol Dyffryn Clwyd a'r Cyffiniau', TRAFODION CYMDEITHAS HANES SIR DDINBYCH, Denbigh, 1952.

Acknowledgements

The author expresses his gratitude to Mr Meic Stephens, his co-editor of the Writers of Wales series, and to Mrs Susan Jenkins of the University of Wales Press for their interest and encouragement.

He acknowledges with thanks the outstanding care and attention with which Mrs Ceinwen Jones has seen the work through the Press.

The Author

Robert Brinley Jones was born in the Rhondda. He was educated there, at the University of Wales (Cardiff) and the University of Oxford (Jesus College). He taught at the University College of Swansea, was Director of the University of Wales Press and was Warden of Llandovery College until 1988. He then worked as a Member of the Broadcasting Standards Council and now serves as a Member of the Board of the British Council. He is Chairman of the Provincial Validating Board for Ministerial Education in the Church in Wales. He is a Fellow of the University of Wales College of Cardiff and an Honorary Fellow of St David's University College, Lampeter.

He has been co-editor, with Meic Stephens, of the Writers of Wales series from its inception in 1970.

Designed by Jeff Clements
Typesetting at the University of Wales Press in 11pt
Palatino and printed in Great Britain by Qualitex
Printing Limited, Cardiff, 1994.

British Library Cataloguing in Publication Data.
A catalogue record for this book is available from the
British Library.

ISBN 0-7083-1235-7

The Publishers wish to acknowledge the financial
assistance of the Welsh Arts Council towards the cost of
producing this volume.